The Reason
for all Existence

How existence at its fundamental level works

The Reason
for all Existence

How existence at its fundamental level works

Davis McLeod

BOOKS

Winchester, UK
Washington, USA

First published by O-Books, 2014
O-Books is an imprint of John Hunt Publishing Ltd., Laurel House, Station Approach,
Alresford, Hants, SO24 9JH, UK
office1@jhpbooks.net
www.johnhuntpublishing.com

For distributor details and how to order please visit the 'Ordering' section on our website.

Text copyright: Davis McLeod 2014

ISBN: 978 1 78279 719 7

Design: Lee Nash

Printed in the USA by Edwards Brothers Malloy

We operate a distinctive and ethical publishing philosophy in all
areas of our business, from our global network of authors to
production and worldwide distribution.

CONTENTS

Introduction

In order to properly examine the reason for existence, not merely human existence but the existence of literally everything, we shall be primarily looking at concepts. More precisely the book will be referring to these specific concepts as the *basic concepts that underpin existence*. The reason for this will be made clear as you continue reading, but suffice to say that all existence depends on these basic concepts to: not only exist in the first place, but to operate in both a logical and familiar fashion.

For any philosophy or science majors this is not to be confused with conceptual analysis. It may in fact be better not to try and relate anything in this book to something that you have previously read. The slate of your 'academic mind' must be as clean as possible, while obviously retaining your logical mind and general 'common sense'. This ensures that you have the best possible chance to understand what is being written on its own merits, without excess baggage being brought along. This not only relates to any emotional attachments to previous ideas in regards to existence and philosophy. It also refers to any word/terminology associations that a reader may have. For instance terms such as 'intuition' or 'concepts' may have very specific (and even non-dictionary defined) meanings for readers, but the way in which this book uses these terms may differ slightly; although obviously this will not apply to every reader. In any case it is important to assign any terms with the description in this book, otherwise some of the meanings within could become lost.

Rather than using overly complicated and unnecessary explanations with a plethora of unfamiliar and academic terminology, this book will try to read as straightforward as possible. Anything worth explaining should be told as simply, with all necessary detail, as possible. Rather than sounding highly technical with the purpose of boosting the ego of the writer, this book aims to be understood by as many people as feasibly possible. This is not to say that some aspects of this book won't be challenging to some degree, but with a little contemplation and by rereading a few sentences or paragraphs, the ideas within should become clear.

Additionally the ideas brought forward in this book are in no way meant to be riddles. It is the ideas themselves that need to be contemplated, rather than any parable or word trickery that may eventually lead to an idea. It would in fact be counter-productive to explain anything within this book in the form of a riddle or in an overly complicated fashion. The reader's full concentration should be on the ideas being put forward, rather than spending time deciphering what those ideas are actually supposed to be in the first place. This could often lead to the reader missing a particular point or, worse yet, the subjective (mis)interpretation of an idea that bears little resemblance to the author's original intent.

Regardless of how straightforward or complex an idea is, everyday examples of the concepts at work will be used to help clarify the ideas being put forward. Simultaneously this will also show how the concepts are directly connected to our actual lives, rather than merely existing in an intellectual void. Additionally there may be some instances where the reader quickly understands the concept they are reading, while there is still a portion of text remaining regarding the concept in question. This is done in order to anticipate some of the main arguments that could be raised with the discussed concepts, rather than an attempt to drag simple ideas out too far.

On the whole this book may in fact seem rather short, especially in regards to its subject matter, but the feeling is that a concise explanation for each idea and concept will suffice. It is then up to the readers themselves to see if these explanations not only match up with the world around them, but also to simple, basic logic. As opposed to certain religious and spiritual ideas, no heightened emotional states or leaps of faith are required to understand the ideas and concepts within. Rather a calm and clear mind is all that is needed.

Concepts

Concepts and Semantics

The concepts discussed within this book, usually referred to as the *basic concepts that underpin existence*, are perhaps obviously expressed in English. This does not necessarily mean that these concepts will be easily understood by everyone whose first language is English. Someone, although likely not famous to any degree, once said that: "Perhaps 1 + 1 does not equal 2 and that we are all wrong. Perhaps 1 + 1 equaled 7, or perhaps an apple, or even something we don't know about yet." Although such a statement might seem ridiculous and many may wonder why it is even in this book, it is an attempt to point out an issue that may affect some readers. The important thing to note is that the terms themselves are not the actual concepts; rather the terms and numerals used within this book are merely representations of the concepts. The concept of 1 + 1 = 2 is just one way of representing this familiar concept. Pushing two almost identical stones together could be considered another more visual way of representing the same concept.

The focus of this book – the *basic concepts that underpin existence* – are all concepts that exist without the need for human or any other living entity's recognition or understanding. All the concepts within this book do not need an individual's intellectual recognition for it to not only affect that individual's life, but also the whole of existence. To make this idea simpler to understand it would be similar to a caveman being unaware that oxygen is affecting his individual life. The caveman's ignorance of oxygen does in no way stop oxygen from affecting the caveman's existence, just because he is almost completely unaware of it. If not already, this idea should be made clearer the further into the book you get.

Concepts or Laws?

As previously mentioned the concepts in the book won't merely be discussed as if they were in a vacuum or far from our everyday experience. The *basic concepts that underpin existence* will always have some effect on our known world as, needless to say, our known world is a part of existence. Therefore these concepts are all apparent in our subjective realities, otherwise known as our everyday lives. As these concepts not only underpin our world, but all of existence, they should be in fact seen as laws, rather than merely subjective ideas. The reason for calling them concepts rather than laws is that we can see the idea of these concepts, but we do not see them in their actuality. The concepts can be explained logically, but to be understood they will need some form of subjective conceptualization from the reader.

For example two such concepts are infinity and pure nothingness (a complete absence of anything). We can logically understand the idea of infinity, but we can never actually witness it in its entirety. If we could it would not actually be infinite. Although we cannot see infinity in its actuality we can imagine, at the very least, the idea of something being without end.

Sometimes we think we are literally witnessing a specific concept, even though we are merely seeing the idea of the concept through our own subjective misconceptions. For instance the concept of pure nothingness seems to appear often, such as: an empty room, the dark void of space, or even the space between molecules. Although there may appear to be literally 'nothing' in certain instances, what we are actually witnessing is merely the idea of pure nothingness, where there is actually something there, but we are unable to recognize it; such as air or something we are yet to discover.

4

Despite this pure nothingness, like infinity, can also be conceptualized even though we cannot literally witness or even form a complete picture of pure nothingness in our minds. Even if we are consciously aware that we cannot literally witness either infinity or pure nothingness we are still able to understand these concepts in principle. This, as you will find, is how all the *basic concepts that underpin existence* work. We can subjectively believe we are witnessing these concepts and understand them conceptually, but we will never witness them in their literal actualities.

Witnessing the Ideas of Concepts Rather Than the Concepts Themselves

It may seem somewhat strange that any *basic concept that underpins existence* can be absolutely true and yet never witnessed in its complete actuality. As broad concepts like infinity and pure nothingness are such 'big' ideas, in a manner of speaking, it may be easier to understand that they cannot be witnessed in their actuality. However, it is likely that there are several slightly less broad concepts that people would be convinced that they see in actuality.

The most obvious example might be the idea of absolute zero (0), as most people would be convinced that absolute zero does exist in our known physical world, at least in certain contexts. Most of us could imagine or believe that we witness absolute zero in regards to something specific; something that we are familiar with in our everyday lives. If someone held out their apparently empty hand we could probably name at least a few thousand things that were not in that hand. Therefore the concept of absolute zero could apply to certain situations in regards to certain things. For example when looking at someone's apparently empty hand it would be plausible to say there was a zero amount of an orange in their hand, and certainly a zero amount of the moon or a zero amount of a dinosaur in their hand.

We will first discuss how this is not actually the case by using the example of an orange, but as you read on you will discover that any example could be used. When someone cuts an orange in two we will see two halves, and four quarters of an orange if those halves are cut in two again. If we kept cutting those orange pieces in half we will most likely see bits of an orange rather than a specific fraction of an orange. When this actually occurs would of course be a subjective observation. It is also a subjective observation when the orange is cut up so often that it no longer resembles any part of an orange at all. In theory if we could keep cutting the pieces of orange forever there would be a point where no human could see any part of the orange at all.

This is not to say that we all have invisible slices of orange in our hands, but it is not that far off the mark. Rather than using fractions it is now perhaps better to use the decimal system. If someone were to say you had 0.0000000000001% of an orange in your hand this may at first seem like a bizarre and pointless thing to say. The truth is there will be something, most likely completely unseen, resting in our hand that could make up some part of an orange. Although no one would dream of calling this any recognizable percentage of an orange, the fact is that oranges like all other things are made up of infinitely smaller objects/things/entities (from now on any object, particle, life-form or anything that could be considered an individual will be referred to as an 'entity' or an 'individual', depending on the context).

This could be something as small as an atom, or any element that we are familiar or unfamiliar with. Although this may sound pedantic, the law of infinity makes this a complete truth. Somewhere on your hand, even right now, or anywhere else for that matter is a building block that can go towards making absolutely anything else. One problem is that some of these building blocks could be beyond our sight or comprehension. As we will discuss throughout the book all of existence stems from the same source, or more specifically the same concepts, therefore everything will, on close enough inspection, consist of the same building blocks.

Even in basic mathematics we see representations of the laws or concepts of mathematics working, rather than the actual mathematics in its purest form. The simplest equation of $1 + 1 = 2$ is something almost everyone is familiar with, and is probably seen unconsciously or consciously by most of us multiple times a day. If we take any two individual cherries in the world and add them together in a bowl, this is an obvious representation of $1 + 1 = 2$. However, both cherries would not be of equal size and therefore they cannot both literally be considered as '1'. If even one of those cherries could be constituted as the pure representation of '1' ideal cherry, the other cherry, even if it were weighed to be exactly the same as the first cherry by human measuring tools, would in fact be different. The second cherry might actually represent 1.00000001 of the supposed ideal cherry, or a number containing several hundred zeroes after the decimal point. On close enough inspection no two cherries would ever be exactly the same.

This applies to everything, whether it was any two of the same factory produced item, any two grains of sand, or any two drops of water. Even if we cannot observe their actual difference, no two individual entities anywhere in the whole of existence will be exactly the same; literally a hundred percent the same. Therefore rather than literally seeing $1 + 1 = 2$ in our known world (including the equation being written or typed), we are seeing a representation of the mathematical concept that $1 + 1 = 2$. We see the idea of the equation rather than the literal equation in its purest form.

Therefore it is not only such broad concepts like infinity and pure nothingness that we merely see the idea of rather than the concept in its actuality, it also applies to any nonhuman made concept, whether it's in regards to: a color, the idea of perfection or any mathematical equation, etc. Additionally the reason why no two entities in the whole of existence can be exactly the same will be made clearer in the following two chapters.

Basic Intuitive Thinking As Opposed to Intuitive Thinking

Before addressing the reason for existence it might be important to address the idea of *basic intuitive thinking*. Although *basic intuitive thinking* is required to understand this book, it does not require any mystical or supernatural talent; it is in fact equivalent to being able to understand the basic concepts of mathematics. Therefore this book should be simplistic enough for anyone of a reasonable age to understand.

Intuition

The term 'intuition', especially to those that see themselves as being extremely rational, can ring the proverbial alarm bell. This is because intuitive thinking in this day and age may often be thought of as: knowing something without apparent rigorous investigation, a lucky guess, irrational, and is often associated with the delusions of a spiritual/religious individual. The idea that the ability to understand any concept is in fact based on, and could only be based upon, intuitive thinking may at first seem like an absolute fallacy.

Intuitive thinking, rather than *basic intuitive thinking*, would be most commonly known as the semi-physic or inspired guesswork that humans do seemingly out of nowhere. For example a brother or sister suddenly knowing that their sibling is in some kind of trouble when they are miles apart and seemingly having no logical reason to have such knowledge. This is not the type of intuition that this book will be referring to. What we will be referring to is the recognition of basic concepts by witnessing the ideas of these concepts in our everyday lives. This might be called 'basic intuition'. A basic intuition that recognizes basic concepts, rather than anything that could be considered psychic or super-natural.

Basic Intuitive Thinking

Basic intuitive thinking involves knowing that a concept is true, rather than just thinking or believing that it is true. Obviously experience and observation increases one's knowledge, which then enables for the better understanding of a particular topic, but what we are specifically discussing is the ability to recognize a complete truth. Once again we can use mathematics to better explain this idea. Mathematics would appear to be based upon reason alone with no intuition needed whatsoever. This could be because basic mathematics is not only used successfully in everyday life; it is also accepted as straightforward and uncontroversial. However, the most important reason would be that individuals will most likely only focus upon the problem solving aspect of mathematics.

An important aspect of mathematics that most people may not consciously think about is understanding the concept of numbers. Recognizing and knowing the concept of '1' is needed before someone can perform basic mathematics. We can see the idea of '1' all around us: 1 cup, 1 grape, 1 person, 1 drop of water. In order to recognize these familiar things we need to first be able to recognize and understand the concept of '1', which must be done with *basic intuitive thinking*.

To explain this idea further the example of $1 + 1 = 2$ will again be used, and although this may be slightly repetitive it's a good way to reiterate certain ideas. Any representation to depict a basic mathematical formula, whether it's the use of pebbles or a language/numeral based representation, will only ever be a representation. If a printer or typewriter were to type the equation: $1 + 1 = 2$, the same amount of ink to type each individual '1' will never be used. Even if it took the world's most powerful microscope this will be found to be the case. This may sound overly fastidious, but it is both accurate and therefore important.

The truth of the matter is that any individual can only be

witness to a representation of any mathematical formula or number. Any mathematical representation will trigger within an individual the knowledge of the actual concept of that mathematical formula or number. It is the recognition and understanding of the concept that occurs, rather than bearing witness to the concept in its actuality. This is *basic intuitive thinking* at work.

If someone witnessed a female and a male lion side by side for the first time, the concept of $1 + 1 = 2$ can be realized even though the two lions are obviously not the same physically. The concept of $1 + 1 = 2$ can be instantly realized with the representation of the two different looking lions if the concept is first understood intuitively. The two objects do not have to appear exactly the same for this concept to be recognized.

Of course it can be argued that humans can be easily convinced that they are seeing the exact, literal representation of this basic mathematical formula. Two grains of sand that look the same with the limitation of human eyes can convince a human that they are in fact observing two identical grains of sand. Even if we did not have the means to observe that the two grains of sand, despite first impressions, were in fact different, it is still the recognition of the concept of 'sameness' or even $1 + 1 = 2$ that actually occurs.

While reason and the analytical mind process equations, the understanding that the basic principles of mathematics are correct must be made intuitively. The use of reason intertwined with intuitive understanding is used to understand and then use concepts, including mathematics, in our everyday lives. To give an example that may be easier to understand in terms of intuitive knowledge is the idea of infinity. As previously mentioned infinity by its nature cannot be observed otherwise it would not truly be infinite. One must first use *basic intuitive thinking* to understand the concept of infinity – in other words to imagine the concept of something never ending, without having to literally visualize something without end.

To then apply that concept to the world/universe we are familiar with requires reason, often involving research, such as understanding that our physical universe can stretch out into infinity by using theoretical physics. If someone did not intuitively understand the concept of infinity they may refuse to believe, or think that a mistake had been made regarding the theory that the physical universe literally stretched out forever. The same can be said about any given number. If someone did not intuitively understand the number '2' any equation involving the number 2 would seem meaningless.

Therefore the form of intuition used here is really the recognition of concepts that underline our very existence. Although these concepts transcend our limited form of existence, despite the world around us triggering the idea of these concepts within us, this form of intuition is still basic in nature. That is to say it is basic in comparison to the complex forms of intuition that resemble something more akin to 'psychic phenomena'. This book does not address these other forms of intuition at all, but that is not to say that other forms of intuition do not exist somewhere in the whole of existence, if not on this very planet.

Life, Creation and Evolution

As this book deals with the reason for existence, it is important to clarify what this book means by existence and how it differs from the idea of 'life' and 'creation'. We will then look at the concept of evolution and how it is connected to the whole of existence. Although evolution is not always considered the same as progression in academia, this book will always consider evolution to be a progression of some kind, while 'regression' will be considered the polar opposite of evolution.

Firstly the idea of 'life' will be thought of as the familiar physical world we know, consisting of anything that most humans subjectively consider to be alive. In other words it is the physical existence of a life-form, whether a human, animal, plant or any other life that goes through the cycle of birth, growth and death. The idea of 'creation', as is commonly known in the realm of metaphysics and theology, consists of some form of creator which has created our known world and presumably worlds unknown.

Existence

The idea of existence put forward in this book transcends not only the life we are familiar with, but also the idea of a creator which, if they existed, has not been adequately explained in terms of how they came to be. Any individual creator, whether human or incorporeal, needs some explanation of why and how they came to be, and how they work. Therefore, life and any theoretical creator of the physical world and universe need to lie within the whole of existence, rather than actually representing existence. The term 'existence' used in this book will literally mean the existence of anything and everything, including that which is unknown to us. Therefore the book's basic aim is to ultimately explain why anything exists at all, and subsequently how existence at its most basic, rudimentary level works. Upon reading the book the reader will understand that the questions of why and how our existence works are in fact inextricably connected.

Although our Earthly lives will be used as examples to help bring forth several ideas concerning the workings of existence, we will not specifically address the idea of 'the meaning of life'. This could be thought of as an individual, subjective matter and often associated with more emotional responses. Having said that the meaning of individual lives would also fall under the umbrella of the 'reason for existence'. This is where under-standing the reason for existence should underpin to some degree the way in which an individual lives their life. The idea of a creator, usually in the form of an omniscient deity, will not be specifically addressed; however, the concepts discussed in this book may help refine or alter one's idea of such a deity.

Evolution as Creation

Two of the most important or common arguments about existence center upon the idea of evolution versus the idea of creation. Although we generally see creation and evolution as separate, if not mutually exclusive, there is a greater connection between the two ideas than many may believe. Generally evolution could be considered as the gradual change of one entity into a completely different entity (although obviously these differences can only ever be viewed subjectively). This is opposed to the idea of creation, which is generally seen as the forming of something new by the deliberate will of one or more intelligent beings.

From these very brief descriptions most of us would then consider a car or an airplane to be a form of creation, as opposed to a stick or a stone. Although some will say that the rudimentary 'design' of sticks and stones were created, the observable process whereby they came about suggests a natural-istic forming. Cars, airplanes, sticks and stones can all have practical uses, but only the first two would usually be considered creations. Paintings and marble sculptures would also be considered creations, as opposed to a unique rock formation or a scenic lake. All four could be judged aesthetically as either beautiful, ugly or anything in between. Once again we would usually only consider the first two as creations, unless religiously inclined in a fundamental or conservative fashion.

To better understand the process of what we would consider to be creation, we will look at several examples. The first is the airplane. Since the airplane's first appearance, its design, like the car or any other piece of technology, has improved significantly over the decades. In other words the design of the airplane has evolved as better ideas and inventions have improved upon its first design. The argument here could be made that each new airplane is more of a new creation, rather than a process of evolution, and that at the very least the very first airplane was an act of creation.

The process of both improving an airplane and creating the first airplane still involves the process of evolution. In fact the design process of any new piece of technology involves evolution whether it is during the drawing boards stage before its 'creation', or in the imagination of the 'creator'. The idea to create an airplane did not pop into someone's head from nowhere; it evolved from a naturalistic origin, such as witnessing a bird fly, or a leaf blowing in the wind. The mind, or the intelligence that imagines such ideas, has also gone through the evolutionary process. The world around us that influences our imaginations and our 'creations', whether it is technology or art, also stems from the process of evolution. In other words the process of evolution affects everything we are familiar with, even that which we perceive as being created.

Therefore any type of 'creation' will in fact contain various forms of evolution. It involves the process of building upon existing ideas through the imagination of an individual or individuals. It involves the evolution of the 'creator' itself in order to give them greater skills and imagination to improve upon previous forms of technology or art. In regards to humans this would also incorporate increases in social knowledge. Finally it also involves the evolutionary process of any influencing factors that are external to the 'creator'.

To those individuals external to the 'creation' process of new artworks or technology, there can be the belief that they are actually witnessing completely new creations. This might occur due to the fact that these apparent 'creations' seem to come about rather quickly, if not almost overnight; especially if they were aesthetically very different to anything the observer had witnessed before. This, like most misconceptions, is due to a lack of awareness and thought. Although the evolutionary process of any artwork or new technology is rarely witnessed by the general population, a little imagination and/or research could give individuals a clearer idea of the origins of supposed new creations.

Growth as Evolution

As we've just discussed, creation is on close examination a form of evolution. Another concept that is considered a form of change, but not necessarily a form of evolution, is the concept of growth. As the concept of growth and evolution will be inextricably linked within this book it is perhaps wise to give a brief reason why we see them as almost one in the same.

To put simply what we may see as growth is actually a display of evolution sped-up, so to speak. To use the consciousness of an individual human as an example, we can see several stages of evolution during the early stages of human life. The elements that make up a human start off with the consciousness of material matter, before progressing to the consciousness of a plant, then an animal, and finally what we would recognize as human consciousness. If we were to look at the importance of evolution in terms of intelligence and consciousness, then it would appear as though the process of human growth displays the evolutionary progress of the species. The important aspect here is not the aesthetic appearance of humans, but the internal progression and the advanced capabilities to grow/evolve even further.

Obviously growth would seem separate to evolution because it appears so much faster than the evolution of a species as a whole. The main reason for this is that the evolutionary progress of humanity (in terms of knowledge and physical experience) is in effect already contained within each newly born individual. This could either be thought of in a purely physical way or metaphysically. This principle works for all entities and even societies. Knowledge within a society that is gained through an individual's rigorous research and contemplation, via academic pursuits for instance, can be far more easily attained by future generations. The difficult process of trial and error to attain new knowledge can be largely bypassed by new generations, leaving more time to improve and expand upon existing knowledge. So too is it with individual humans. As the basic attributes of the human physique and consciousness have been attained previously, a new child does not need to go through all those long and rigorous evolutionary processes again. Any aspect of human growth, whether it's the growth of the eyes or the ability to use language, is all derived from the past evolutionary progress of the species. In effect any form of growth is built upon and cannot exist without evolution.

Although we are yet to explain how the concept of evolution works and its relationship to existence, it is important to know that it refers to the positive change, gradual or otherwise, of individual entities. Any form of change, whether we generally consider such change to be creation, growth or any other occurrence, is all to be considered either evolution or regression.

Chapter 1

Existence from Void

Unlike everything we are familiar with in our known physical world, nothing or more accurately the concept of 'pure nothingness' does not have a prior cause, as nothing can literally create pure nothingness. This is because it is merely the absence of anything; it is an absolute void. Pure nothingness, rather than a conventional explanation of its 'existence', needs to be defined.

The way in which anything, including the concept of pure nothingness, is properly defined is due to its juxtaposition to something that is different. In the physical world individual entities are defined by their surroundings which are different in texture, color and form. If everything was literally the same in regards to texture, color and form, then existence would be hard to fathom. Every entity or concept is different in order to define itself as its own unique 'individual'. Anything that is observable as an individual, whether it is a tree, a person or a grain of sand, is defined not only by its own unique characteristics, but also by the uniqueness of surrounding entities.

In simple terms the concept of pure nothingness exists due to its juxtaposition to 'something'. Something and nothing define one another, therefore without pure nothingness there could not be something and vice versa. Even in the physical world the idea of nothing and something coexist. The 'space' in between individual entities, which can be initially perceived as a form of nothingness, allows for individual entities to appear. If there were no perceived space in between individual entities then the idea of individualism as we know it would not exist. There would rather just be one solid mass. Several of these concepts, such as pure nothingness, individualism and why things appear different, will be discussed in greater depth as the book unfolds.

All *basic concepts that underpin existence* are in fact defined by their exact opposites. Therefore it is not just anything that can accurately define the concept of pure nothingness; it is something more specific. In a way it is similar to someone saying that 1 is the opposite of 0. The issue here is that there could be an equal argument that 2, 100 or even 42 could be the opposite of 0, as they are all numbers rather than the absence of a number. In actual fact it is the concept of infinity (∞ this symbol will be used to represent the numeral definition of infinity from now on) that defines the concept of 0, as they are absolute opposites.

Similar to the concepts of 0 and ∞ defining each other, the concept of pure nothingness needs to be defined by its complete and absolute opposite, rather than just merely 'anything'. The simple answer is that the complete opposite of pure nothingness is the most perfect 'something', which this book will define as 'Infinitum Perfectus'. Infinitum Perfectus can be thought of as infinite perfection; infinite in size and completely perfect.

Infinity and Infinitum Perfectus

Infinity

Before discussing the concept of Infinitum Perfectus further it is important to briefly address the concept of infinity, as it is an integral part of Infinitum Perfectus. One must understand that infinity is not merely represented by the immensity of the known universe; outer space, but also inner space. Infinity would not be infinite if it did not go both ways, so to speak. This incorporates the idea of the infinitely large and the infinitely small. These concepts can be hard to grasp as there is a limit to what human sight and consciousness can perceive. Currently the smallest individual entities known to humanity lie within the world of the subatomic. Aside from what can exist in our own imagination, the largest entities known to us exist in the far reaches of space. Although obviously such immense bodies, whether a quasar, star or a planet, are all made up of smaller entities.

The idea of the infinitely large and the infinitely small effectively means that there cannot be a smallest nor a largest individual entity in the entirely of existence. Imaging such an idea could leave one utterly perplexed. It is conceivable that one may be able to imagine something perpetually increasing in size in theory, but to imagine that something was able to shrink for all eternity may seem absurd. Usually the idea of something perpetually shrinking lends to the belief that that entity would eventually disappear into nothingness. From our limited perspective that would indeed appear true, but in reality something could indeed shrink endlessly without literally disappearing into pure nothingness.

To help understand such a puzzling idea we will once again look at mathematics. Of course one could immediately claim that 1 was the lowest number and that 0 in fact represented pure nothingness, but thanks to the decimal system we know this is not entirely true. Similar to the infinite amount of whole numbers one could have in mathematics, there are also an infinite amount of decimal numbers. This is due to the fact that there is no theoretical limit on the number of zeroes that can be placed after the decimal point. This can effectively create a pattern where every number, whole or decimal, is made up of even smaller numbers.

For instance the decimal number 0.01 is made up of ten 0.001s, while the decimal number 0.001 is made up of ten 0.0001s, and so it goes. This pattern we find in numbers can be applied to everything else, whether it is physical matter or energy. Every entity is made up of smaller entities, which are in turn made up of even smaller entities and so on. This must be thought of as a perpetual pattern, whether an individual can subjectively observe this or not.

Although imagining an infinitely shrinking entity that never literally disappears into nothingness or even an entity made up of an infinite number of smaller entities may seem strange, there is something even stranger about the concept of infinity. There actually appear to be two types of infinity. Although logically only one 'thing' should be considered infinite, as infinity by its definition should encompass everything else, otherwise it is not truly infinite. There is, however, cause to believe otherwise.

To help understand this strange idea of multiple infinities we shall once again look at basic mathematics. The idea basically stems from the fact that, as previously mentioned, an infinite number of numerical digits can be placed after the decimal point, as there is no mathematical law to prevent this. This then allows for an infinite amount of decimal numbers in mathematics. Irrational numbers, with perhaps the number of pi (π) being the most famous, are a case in point where the number of digits after the decimal point is literally endless. Therefore each individual whole number (this would also apply to any decimal number), such as the number 1, contains within it an infinite amount of decimal numbers.

Therefore anything that could be considered as a whole, whether it was a number or an individual entity, would in fact contain infinity within. As long as there is no smallest entity, where literally everything is made up of something smaller, then the idea of infinity can exist inside of anything. If we look at mathematics once again, as it may be easier for the reader to visualize, we can see that there are bizarrely an infinite number of infinities. This is due to the fact that there are an infinite amount of whole numbers, each containing an infinite amount of decimal numbers. As existence in actuality is also infinite, then there would be an infinite number of entities made up of an infinite number of smaller entities. Therefore existence, like mathematics, appears to be made up of an infinite number of infinities.

If the idea of infinity is supposed to literally incorporate everything then it may appear to make little sense that infinity exists within every single individual entity. This is in part one of the reasons that the concept of Infinitum Perfectus exists separate to the concept of infinity. Infinitum Perfectus includes the infinite number of infinities, and thereby truly encompasses everything.

Infinitum Perfectus

There has been a tendency in modern academia to use Latin on occasion, perhaps most notably in the field of biology in regards to naming organisms (their scientific name rather than their common name). This is most likely done so organisms share the same name worldwide, as common names for organisms usually differ throughout the Earth's various cultures. Latin names are also used in other fields of academia such as law, mathematics and other science disciplines besides biology. If anything a Latin name adds a degree of prestige, which can be missing from its English translation. This can look rather common due to its familiarity in our everyday language. Therefore in attempting to name something new, at least in terms of naming a concept that might seem unfamiliar to a large majority of readers, we have decided to use the term: Infinitum Perfectus to describe a very specific idea, as the English translation of 'perfect infinity' or 'infinite perfection' may not adequately evoke a special meaning to the readers.

Infinitum Perfectus in this book not only means an infinite number of infinites. Infinitum Perfectus to put simply also means that every individual entity, of which there are an infinite number, has reached its utmost potential and become literally perfect. If every aspect, every part of existence that was once individualized finally evolved into perfection, then there would no longer be any individual forms of existence; only one uniform, perfect form of existence that truly stretched out into infinity. This is Infinitum Perfectus.

Pure Nothingness

Something that would be considered infinitely perfect may not at first seem to be the exact opposite of pure nothingness for one reason. When we look at the concept of pure nothingness, as observing pure nothingness in actuality is impossible (even in our imagination something always appears when we try to imagine pure nothingness), we might at first consider it to be boundless and infinite. This could be due to two main ideas. One is that there is nothing that can confine pure nothingness in any way, therefore pure nothingness would seem to expand into infinity. The other idea is from the old-fashioned notion, possibly still held by some, that outer space is an actualization of pure nothingness, which from our subjective point of view can appear infinite in scope.

In fact the truth is that the concept of pure nothingness would not be infinite as it requires no space to occupy. Pure nothingness must be thought of as not an empty space with specific dimensions, but in actual fact a complete absence of anything. There are no dimensions to pure nothingness at all. It is in fact anti-infinity – in mathematical terms it would be absolute zero (0), the opposite of ∞. Therefore pure nothingness is the exact opposite to Infinitum Perfectus in every aspect.

The Eternal Journey to Infinitum Perfectus

The Reality of Infinitum Perfectus and Perfection

There is now most likely one obvious question on your mind. How could Infinitum Perfectus possibly be real when there appears to be no current material evidence for this? If every entity within Infinitum Perfectus was indeed the most perfect it could possibly be then this would suggest uniformity, with all individuals becoming indistinct from one another.

The immediate issues here are that not only do we exist in a world where distinctness can be found anywhere and everywhere, but there is also a grave lack of 'perfection'. In fact one's imagination is most likely able to envision a world far better than the one we currently inhabit. Therefore when we juxtapose this world, or even our known universe, with the concept of pure nothingness they do not appear as polar opposites. Even though subjectively we may witness great beauty in this world, it would appear as though we are a random patchwork of imperfect entities. To understand why we don't seem to perceive objective perfection in our everyday lives, we must closely look at the concept of perfection itself.

The concept of perfection is similar to the concept of the color white, which is in no way to be confused with the racial term 'white'. On many occasions one may think that they have gazed upon a surface that appears to be perfectly white, without a blemish or hint of any other color. When one closely examines what they think to be the purest white surface they will discover, even if requiring a microscope, that the white surface is far from perfectly white. The surface will contain blemishes and shades of other colors strewn between speckles of white. Even those patches of white within the surface would not be perfectly white on even closer inspection.

With our unaided, natural eyesight the surface will still appear to be pure white. The same is true with the idea of perfection. The idea of perfection can be observed by an individual in one particular instance, but this perception will not last forever. After some time the advancement and greater experience of the individual will change their expectations of what they subjectively consider to be 'perfection'. The individual will raise the bar on what they consider to be perfection, so to speak. If an individual's idea of perfection can continually be refined there would then be the question of whether objective perfection can actually be achieved. If Infinitum Perfectus were to ever be observed it would require the concept of objective perfection to be an actuality.

Perfection as an Endless Journey

A child may one day learn of the existence of the number 1,000,000, and for an instance this may seem like the largest number conceivable. Upon further investigation if each of the digits were changed to a 9 then for another instance this may seem like the largest number. The curious mind would doubtless not stop there and by adding another number, or even another digit (taking us to the tens of millions), the highest number would again increase. The individual would then realize there is likely no highest number in actuality as any number, if one's imagination, or space on their computer or notepad will allow, can continually be added to. This of course is where the idea of ∞ comes from. Infinity (∞) could be thought of as: *the highest number + 1*. If this were an actual equation it would accurately describe the perpetual and endless nature of all existence and not just merely the concept of ∞ as a mathematical term.

Just as there is no way to limit the amount of whole (or decimal) numbers that can exist in mathematics, there is no actual way to limit anything else. Limitations are only found in particular contexts with imperfect and subjective observations, such as humanity's limited ability to witness the physical cosmos. Similar to the idea that the highest possible number can never literally be reached, the idea of perfection would also be literally unobtainable, as there is no way to limit how perfect/better something can be. The law of infinity will ultimately prevent any individual experiencing Infinitum Perfectus, as perfection itself is a never-ending, eternal journey.

To better highlight the idea of perfection as an eternal journey we will once again use mathematics as a metaphor. Firstly we will consider any whole number to represent the idea of individual perfection, while any decimal number is an individual that has yet to achieve perfection. The higher the decimal number the closer that individual is to perfection. Each decimal number's journey is to become a whole number; in other words an individual's journey to perfection. For each individual to reach the ultimate in perfection (a whole number) they must first pass through every decimal number.

As there are an infinite amount of decimal numbers the journey to a whole number would be eternal; literally never ending. It is obviously difficult to visualize or to even conceptualize the idea of passing through every possible decimal number, as there is literally no smallest decimal number to begin counting from. Even if we were to start at any given decimal number there would still be an endless number of decimal numbers we would need to count. This is then the point – which will be elaborated on further in the section: *Instantaneous and Infinite Existence* – it is not possible to reach a whole number if one had to count every single decimal number, as it is also impossible for any individual to reach ultimate perfection.

As humans we could not even adequately assign ourselves a metaphorical decimal number to illustrate our progress towards perfection. Any such self-assessment would be subjective and ultimately futile. If we are honest with ourselves, no matter how far we were to advance as individuals, or even as a human race, we could only feel as though we were roughly in the middle of our journey. Even if we could sustain our physical bodies and live eternal lives as individual personalities, we would still, unless deliberately deluding ourselves, feel this sensation. As we evolve and our perceptions advance, our notion of perfection would continually improve, becoming loftier and loftier, but it would always be out of reach. Although one might find this idea objectionable, or just rather bizarre, this is the only way existence could ever be.

The concept of objective perfection may never be witnessed, just as pure nothingness may also never be witnessed. Nevertheless those concepts remain true, just as the concept of infinity is true, but can never be witnessed by a single entity. So it is with Infinitum Perfectus.

Instantaneous and Infinite Existence

If the concept of Infinitum Perfectus is true then logically it should always have existed, and it should continue to exist for all eternity. This is due to the concept of pure nothingness being eternal. Pure nothingness cannot have a beginning as it is an absolute absence of anything and therefore, as previously mentioned, does not need explaining; it merely requires a definition. In short if the concept of pure nothingness is eternal and defines and is defined by Infinitum Perfectus, then the concept of Infinitum Perfectus must also be eternal and literally without beginning. Therefore whatever makes up Infinitum Perfectus must also be eternal.

The Existence of Everything

As existence, including the world and universe we're familiar with, must logically lie in between pure nothingness and Infinitum Perfectus this would then suggest that everything conceivable, every form of existence, has literally always existed. For many this idea could be hard to grasp, as the majority of humanity would think that most, if not all things, should have a beginning. To use a simple analogy the concept or laws of mathematics (numbers) work in the same fashion. The concept of 0 and ∞ will always exist, as they are clearly concepts that require no physical manifestation to exist and remain true. Therefore as these two mathematical concepts (0 and ∞) define one another, then every single conceivable number between these two mathematical concepts must have also always existed. If any number ceased to exist (although impossible) then ∞ could not exist (also impossible), as it would no longer be infinite.

This same pattern works for all *basic concepts that underpin existence*. For example the concepts of black and white also define each other. Therefore the concept of every color or spectrum of light in between black and white will also simultaneously exist. This is because (in terms of light) white contains all of the possible colors that could conceivably exist. If one spectrum of light (or color) suddenly ceased to exist (although impossible) white could not exist (also impossible). The pattern here should be obvious concerning all concepts that represent a complete absence which define their opposites, such as: pure nothingness, 0, and black. White and ∞ contain every possible color and number respectively, so then the concept of Infinitum Perfectus must follow suit.

Obviously the idea that all existence, both known and unknown, has always existed would immediately raise an issue for most people. Logically one would say that humans, animals and even plant life have not always existed in the physical world/universe we are familiar with. The law of infinity, however, dictates that somewhere in the whole of existence there would be entities with the consciousness of humans, animals and plant life at any given moment. Even after evolutionary factors have transformed humanity (and any other entity for that matter) into something unfamiliar, there would somewhere in the whole of existence still be present entities that are similar to our current state. Although to say that somewhere in the whole of existence there will be an exact replica of how you were 5 years ago (or any other instance) would not be entirely accurate. This specific idea will be discussed further in the subsection: *How Everything is Different Without a Beginning.*

Perhaps the most difficult issue for many readers to comprehend is how everything conceivable not only existed at the very same time as each other, but that they had always existed. One of the major reasons for this is the obvious discrepancies between the advancement of individual entities, both in terms of physical properties, and more importantly in their level of consciousness. If everything had simultaneously existed and had always existed in some form or another, this would then seem like a paradox. Although there are laws in regards to cause and effect, which form evolution and cause change, this in itself might not adequately explain why certain entities are far more evolved than others. This will also soon be addressed in the subsection: *How Everything is Different Without a Beginning*. For the moment we will briefly address the common assumption that everything has a first cause, which would put into question the idea that everything has always existed in some form or another.

Humanity has always observed an array of causes that have formed any individual entity. Therefore it would have stood to reason that there was a first cause, an original cause that has allowed for all that follows. The idea that only a concept, the ultimate dichotomy of pure nothingness and Infinitum Perfectus, has allowed for such an abundance of diversity without a literal first cause may seem baffling. If rigorous thought is applied, minus any attachment to previous held beliefs, a first cause to all of existence cannot literally cause itself out of nothing 'all of a sudden'. The idea that a spark of life randomly appeared out of nothing as a first cause, apparently on a whim, refutes simple logic.

Even though the idea that all of existence had always existed, albeit not exactly in the form humanity is currently familiar with, could be hard to fathom, it is the only logical explanation for existence. Any other explanation does not reside in the world of logic; it is merely an emotional yearning based upon personal insecurities, or a simple misconception based on confusion. There can only ever be a law to explain the whole of existence. The reliance of any 'first cause' to explain the whole of existence will inevitably need a law to explain the origins of this first cause in any case.

The important thing to remember is that the fundamental concepts of pure nothingness and Infinitum Perfectus are the reason for each other's existence; therefore one does not come before the other and neither can exist by itself. There can be no beginning for either. Once again the concept of pure nothingness cannot be caused by anything – it cannot have a prior cause, so as a concept it is impossible for it to not 'exist'. As with all concepts, pure nothingness cannot exist without its complete opposite to define it, so it is also literally impossible for Infinitum Perfectus to not exist. Therefore, like pure nothingness and Infinitum Perfectus, all of existence, which lies in between these two concepts, is literally eternal.

Any form of 'beginning', any at all, is purely subjective. No matter what appears to have come out of nowhere, whether it was: an earthquake, a thought, a universe, a work of art or anything beyond human comprehension, there will always be a lead up to any perceived beginning.

How Everything is Different Without a Beginning

As previously mentioned one apparent issue with the idea that 'nothing that ever exists has a beginning', in terms of appearing from pure nothingness, is that everything is different. What is specifically meant by this is that not everything has evolved or developed to the same degree. This may immediately seem strange as all of existence has come from the same source, being the fundamental concepts of pure nothingness and Infinitum Perfectus.

Obviously we are limited in what we can observe, but by just examining the life on Earth there are vast differences among the various life-forms. Plant life is not as evolved as animals, animals are less evolved than humans (although some may argue differently) and, even within humans, individuals are far from equal in terms of intelligence, consciousness and physical prowess. As there were no 'head-starts' for any individual entity in the process of evolution, there needs to be a logical explanation for the discrepancies in terms of evolutionary progress between individuals.

There are several things that need to be addressed in order to answer this question. One is our notion of time. We may at first think that if two very similar entities are subjected to the exact same experience/conditions for the same amount of time, then they will simultaneously have the same reactions as each other. For instance someone might assume that putting two almost identical ice cubes in a heated frying pan for the same amount of time will cause the ice cubes to melt at the same rate. This will not happen, as it is not the human concept of time that determines the rate and degree of change to any individual entity. It is a combination of the different internal reactions of the two ice cubes, and the fact that the external influence upon the two ice cubes is also different.

The two ice cubes in the heated frying pan will actually experience slightly different levels of heat, no matter how hard anyone attempts to make the spread of heat completely even. There will always be discrepancies with the level of heat, even if we are unable to detect those differences. The two ice cubes will also be different to some degree, which will also affect the rate in which they melt. Once again this is true whether we are able to detect such differences or not.

This of course does not answer the underlying question of how the ice cubes and external influences (uneven spread of heat) came to be different in the first place, but it can offer a clue. The reason that any individual entity is and has always been different follows the same idea as the ultimate reason for existence. Individual entities are not defined by their complete opposite in the same way that basic concepts are defined. Individual entities that exist in actuality are in fact defined in some way by every other entity. So rather than an individual entity being the literal opposite of everything else, they are instead completely unique in comparison to all other entities.

As any entity has the potential to encounter a vast number of other entities it will continually be defined, thus allowing for its continued change and uniqueness. As everything is literally different, even if such differences cannot be detected by a particular individual, no two entities will encounter or experience the exact same external influences in exactly the same way.

The reason for this is that no two individual entities will literally encounter the exact same entities (external influences) at the exact same instance, therefore leading to slightly different encounters. For instance if two brothers encountered the same elderly man, they would be subject to a slightly different reaction from the elderly man. This would be true even if one brother greeted the elderly man a split second before the other brother. The only way the brothers could encounter the elderly man at the exact same instance was if there were literally in the exact same space. Obviously this cannot happen. The fact that the brothers themselves would at least be minutely different would also trigger a slightly different reaction from the elderly man.

Although the reactions from the elderly man may almost be the same, if not completely indistinguishable by our standards, his reactions towards the brothers will never actually be the exact same. If nothing else the encounter with the first brother will alter the elderly man's state of mind and emotional state somewhat. Then the encounter with the second brother a split second later will be slightly different, even if it is only by a small degree due to the influence of seeing the first brother. Although this example suggests only a minute change of reaction, they are changes nevertheless. There of course will be many instances where the changes in reactions are far greater.

Whether large or small, there will always be different reactions within each individual as no entity would encounter another entity in the exact same way, due to those encountered entities constantly changing themselves through the same process. This will be elaborated on further at the beginning of the next chapter, in the section: *Flux*. Therefore no two entities that are (or appear to be) separate in any way will form in the exact same way, as their external influences will always be different. Although this would be hard for us as humans to constantly witness – in fact it may rarely be observed by some individuals – it is the only logical way that everything can be and has always been different without a beginning. As existence is 'infinitely long', such small differences in individual experiences will eventually lead to large discrepancies in the development of individual entities. This of course is the reason why we live in a world where the development of life-forms is so varied.

As only the concept of Infinitum Perfectus can entail an existence where everything is the same, in the form of complete oneness and perfection, then some form of difference between all individual entities will always exist. Once again this is due to the fact that perfection is never achievable in actuality. If there were a finite number of entities there would be a limited gap between the least and most evolved individuals. As there are an infinite number of individual entities in the entirety of existence, there would literally be an infinite gap between the least and most evolved entities.

* * *

As this chapter *Existence from Void* has illustrated, pure nothingness and Infinitum Perfectus are the very fundamentals to existence. At its most simplest, existence could be thought of as perpetually growing out of the void of pure nothingness into the infinite perfection of Infinitum Perfectus.

Although the other *basic concepts that underpin existence* are in a way secondary to the fundamental concepts of pure nothingness and Infinitum Perfectus, they are nevertheless important. The remainder of the book will now look at some of these concepts, as they are not only important in establishing a pattern of how existence works, but they can also be connected with our everyday lives.

Chapter 2

A Fluid Existence

Flux

The term 'flux' used in this book simply refers to ongoing change and movement, and not to be confused with its usage in the disciplines of mathematics or physics. In our everyday lives we constantly witness various forms of change, which often appear sporadic rather than constant. When closely examining the way in which existence operates (even in our known physical existence) it should be seen that change and movement are in fact constant, rather than sporadic.

Stagnation and Constant Movement

To suggest that absolutely everything is in a constant state of flux might at first seem completely false, as one could only imagine a world filled with chaos if everything were constantly changing. On further contemplation the realization should be made that any appearance of sudden change is due to much smaller changes that are unnoticed by our limited human perceptions. Those smaller unnoticed changes are in turn due to even smaller changes and so it goes. If we could examine anything close enough we would be able to witness movement at some level. There will always be movement within each individual entity – not merely repetitive movement, but movement that eventually leads to change visible to external entities. This may often appear subjectively slow to us, but nevertheless there will always be change within any given entity, leading to of course the idea of an existence in constant flux.

Obviously with our everyday perceptions we often witness what appears to be short-term and long-term stagnation, most often in regards to nonliving matter and to some degree plant life. Any individual entity can display the idea of stagnation to the subjective viewer, but as with all basic concepts only the idea is observed, rather than the concept of stagnation or absolute stillness in its actuality.

In this regard the idea of movement is not strictly observed either, rather only the idea of movement is observed. It is the recognition of change that is observed, such as the different heights of a growing tree or the different locations of a flying bird in the sky. No matter how improved an individual's perception becomes, the actual process of movement is not observed, merely a greater ability at witnessing change. Needless to say the concept of movement is real, otherwise change would not occur.

Change and Subjective Identification

One important aspect in regards to an existence that is in constant flux is that it can raise questions about the way humanity subjectively identifies entities. As we've discussed previously the perfection of the whole of existence is not possible, but this also applies to what we will call purely human made concepts. Many of these concepts are the labels given to what we subjectively consider to be the same type of entity, for example a specific species of animal. An example of this is the concept of a gorilla. This is not to be confused with the term 'gorilla', but what we subjectively consider a gorilla to be beyond its linguistic label. From our point of view gorillas are not only similar enough to each other to be considered one type of entity, the gorillas themselves seem to behave as though they are the same type of entity. Although there are now more scientific ways in which to group types of animals/species, traditionally these two reasons were often enough to consider such animals to be one type of entity.

Many of us may have a specific idea of what the 'perfect gorilla' should represent, most likely in terms of physical appearance and behavior. The fact is that any entity that we as humans observe is merely something that is in flux, rather than any form of perfection. In other words there is no perfect idea of a gorilla or anything else subjectively labeled by humanity. Therefore gorillas are not on any journey to becoming perfect gorillas. Rather any given gorilla should be thought of as an entity that is part of the infinity of existence on its never-ending journey to the idea of overall perfection. This is the case for all entities.

Although everything is in a state of flux, the limited ability in which the majority (if not all) of humanity can identify the results of this continual flux creates the notion of stability. Therefore we are able to successfully label entities as a specific type of entity. The thought that gorillas are even now still evolving might not occur to us as they appear, more or less, the same as last year and most likely decades prior. Each gorilla on close inspection will of course be different, but their funda-mental principles, at least to us, appear the same.

As the entities we call gorillas are in fact in a constant state of flux, we could also look at the concept of gorillas as something that is in between two other human made concepts. The next part, although potentially confusing to some, is important to help establish two main ideas about existence. That nothing we perceive in actuality, as opposed to any *basic concept that underpins existence*, is set in stone, and that although everything is in constant flux, individual subjectivism will still allow for a sense of stability.

Here we will use the idea of evolution by natural selection, as it may at least be recognizable to most readers, whether they agree with it or not. To most of humanity a gorilla would be seen as the concept that lies in between the concept of a monkey and the concept of a human. To further explain we will use mathe-matics as a metaphor to describe a gorilla as the numbers between 4.5–5.5. The number 5 in this instance is the concept of a gorilla that is equally as far away from the concept of a monkey as it is from the concept of a human. The number 4.5 would then be the idea of a gorilla that is the closest to a monkey, while still remaining a gorilla in the subjective eyes of a human. The number 5.5 is therefore a gorilla most similar to a human before it is no longer subjectively viewed as a gorilla. This is not to say that 5 equals the gorilla in its most perfect form; rather it represents the middle ground of what humans subjectively identify as a monkey on one side and a human on the other.

Continuing on with this mathematical metaphor another far more advanced being with superior powers of observation may observe what we call gorillas as three distinct types of entities: 4.5–4.83 as one type of entity, 4.84–5.16 as another and 5.17–5.5 as yet another. This is not to say that the entity (which we would still consider to be a gorilla) magically becomes something else when it steps from 4.83 to 4.84. It is merely a metaphor for when the subjective observer is able to witness enough change to distinguish between what appears to be two different types of entities.

Even between different humans change will be viewed subjectively. This has to do with the power of observation, which is not only limited to sight, but could also include the ability to witness the gradual change in someone's personality and character; including both mood swings and more permanent changes. Two humans may witness the igniting of a match at almost the same time; but when witnessing the growth rate of a child, one individual may notice a difference a day, or even a week earlier than the other individual. Therefore we should see that the subjective observation of change involves not only the level of change to the entity in question, but also the ability of the observer.

Our own evolutionary progress influences how we observe and group other entities, along with when and how we recognize change. Therefore although there is constant flux within everything, an individual's observational limitations create the illusion of stagnation and the subjective idea of how fast and sporadic change occurs. The reasons behind the concept of movement and why things 'speed up' will be addressed in the section: *Evolution*, specifically the subsection: *Speed of Movement*.

Evolution

In the context of this book the process of evolution involves two major concepts: size and speed. This will specifically entail the idea of expansion (the increase of size), and the increasing speed of movement. What expansion/growth and speed of movement have to do with evolution will be made clearer throughout this entire chapter, rather than being answered within this section alone. These two concepts, such as the fundamental concepts of pure nothingness and Infinitum Perfectus, exist beyond the world we know. This simply means that even if humanity or this entire world no longer existed, these concepts would remain eternal.

In regards to the idea of growth, or expansion, there is the potential to think that as existence is infinite it must be forever expanding. From an individual entity's perspective the physical universe or even existence beyond the physical may seem to perpetually expand. All that is actually growing is the perceptive abilities of the observer. If existence has and will always be infinite it cannot actually expand any further, otherwise it would not be infinite; there would in effect be no 'space' left to expand into.

What actually expands are the individual entities within existence. Although this would suggest that if individual entities expanded then surely the whole of existence would also have to expand. How and why this happens without actually expanding the entirety of existence will soon be explained.

Growth and Individualism

Before addressing one of the ideas regarding expansion or growth that most humans are familiar with: that bigger is not necessarily better, we will first look at the concept of growth and how it is connected to the concept of individualism. This may seem like an arbitrary exercise, but it is in fact connected with the idea of how individuals can grow in size while the whole of existence does not.

Growth is usually thought of, in its most simplistic terms, as the using of lesser elements/entities to help add to another, usually more evolved entity. Of course this is material/physical growth from the human perspective and can be seen in all living life-forms. Celestial bodies arguably follow a similar process, as their gravitational pull brings together much smaller elements to create the massive bulks that eventually form the stars, planets and their moons. What we are specifically looking at, rather than the scientific explanation of how material entities increase in size, is the philosophical explanation of why growth occurs. Although as you read on you will find that these two ideas are not that dissimilar.

For Infinitum Perfectus to eventuate it must transform all lesser forms of existence to create a single entity of perfection. As we've previously explained this process occurs through individual entities defining and reacting to one another through an endless process, resulting in the evolution or growth of individuals. One of the most important aspects of growth is the recognition that something is in fact an individual; otherwise growth cannot occur. Something that reacts as if it were an individual has the capacity to grow even further than its current state of being. If something no longer saw itself as an individual it would fall apart rather than grow, as the concept of flux does not allow for true stagnation. Therefore something either grows or it deteriorates (evolves or regresses), and any perceived stagnation is subjective due to the limitations of the observer. Although this might all seem straightforward there is in fact an underlying issue with the idea of individualism.

From our (unscientific) perspective a single drop of water and a single grain of sand would seem like true individual entities.

On closer inspection, whether we're looking at a grain of sand or a mountain, all things are made up of smaller, separate parts. The issue here is that if all individual entities are made up of smaller entities, which are themselves to some degree all different, then how does anything appear to be a whole, and how could anything possibly grow? If nothing is really a whole entity, as everything is only made up of smaller and smaller entities, then it might seem that things should fall apart rather than grow, as everything is merely a collection of separate entities.

The ability to see a whole individual entity is due to two factors. One is the subjectivity of the observer and the other, which might seem bizarre at first, is that of the observed: the individual itself. Both of these are required if anything or anyone were to ever appear as a whole individual entity. Firstly, from a human perspective, the observer must see not only atoms but also much larger elements as so similar that they appear to form one whole entity. Obvious examples would be the ocean, an animal, another human, a grain of sand, or even the leaves of a tree could be seen as individual entities. This, however, is not enough to generate the idea of individual entities. All the parts of any individual entity must see themselves and cooperate as if there were a whole; in other words a collective must subjectively believe it's an individual.

Subjective Individualism

When individual entities react against/define themselves in opposition to other entities, many of these individuals will inevitably evolve in a similar fashion – similar in comparison to other surrounding entities. Similar enough in fact that they are able to interact as if they were one larger whole entity. As no individual entity will achieve perfection their perceptive abilities will also never be perfect. Therefore when comparing a collective that appears so similar in comparison to surrounding entities there can be a sense that one is witnessing or experiencing (subjective) individualism.

Unfortunately we are limited in what we can observe, but we can see this play out in our known world on several levels. Individual cells cooperate in the Earth's various life-forms and work as one, rather than split apart to become truly individual-istic. Species often work as one group in order to greater benefit themselves, as they see themselves as one group of very similar individuals compared to other surrounding individuals. When a species, humans are a prime example, inflict pain upon each other it is because they either: see their specific tribe/group as separate from other groups, or they see themselves as completely separate from all other individuals and act selfishly. Obviously the closer in similarity individuals see themselves and surrounding individuals the more likely they are to see themselves as being one, rather than separate.

Therefore as a basic concept growth, or expansion, occurs when increasing numbers of evolving entities appear so similar to other evolving entities that they see themselves and behave as one individual. So in actuality what we observe and what other entities react to is the illusion of sameness that creates individual entities. This, as humans and even animals have shown, can be done consciously in the form of seeing and behaving as though one tribe or nation is a single whole. This is obviously done less effectively than viewing the body/personality as the individual, but with further evolution this would gradually change.

This also explains why individual entities can grow and expand while the whole of existence does not. Nothing grows by conjuring extra material/energy out of 'thin air' (pure nothingness), so to speak. Everything that goes towards the growth of any individual entity already comes from within existence; nothing else is created. What is actually occurring is the journey to Infinitum Perfectus. Before Infinitum Perfectus is theoretically reached, the process of all entities coming together to form one infinitely perfect existence or 'being' must take place.

Therefore any expanding, evolving individual is in effect going through a microcosm of the process that will theoretically allow for Infinitum Perfectus to occur. The journey to Infinitum Perfectus will continually see individual entities come together in order to expand and evolve.

The reason why continued growth, rather than stagnation, occurs is that the infinity of existence contains an infinite number of individual entities. Therefore the concept of growth for all individual entities is inevitable as there will always more and more individual entities that have evolved in a similar way to see themselves as one whole. There will also simultaneously be enough entities that are sufficiently different from one another. This ensures the constant process of individual entities defining themselves in opposition to those that are noticeably (subjectively) different, thereby allowing for the continued process of evolution.

Physical Dimensions

The concept of growth, or expansion, also brings about what we refer to as the three dimensions: length, width and height. This of course also refers to direction itself, whether we think of it as: north, south, east, west; or perhaps more appropriately: forwards, backwards, up, down, left and right. Of course every other possible direction lies in between these commonly known directions.

This not only allows for 'space' which is important for growth, but also movement, which is just as important to generate the experiences required for growth. The thing to realize in regards to the physical dimensions is that they did not exist before or because of the concept of growth, but simultaneously with the concepts of growth and evolution. Growth is impossible without the concept of dimensions and every single possible direction, while physical dimensions would not exist without growth, because without growth there would only be pure nothingness.

As with everything else, dimensions, or more specifically every direction, is defined by its opposite: if there is up there is down, if there is backwards there is forwards, and if there is right there is left. More accurately it should be thought that the concept of 'no direction at all', defines every possible direction. The concept of 'no direction at all' cannot define one direction, as in theory there is no 'best' direction that is the complete opposite of no direction. As all possible directions are theoretically equal, the concept of 'no direction at all' must define all possible directions.

Therefore if a direction is theoretically possible we as individuals can subjectively experience it. As any individual can experience anything from every possible direction they will inevitably react and grow in every possible direction as a result. This then allows for what we observe as the three-dimensional world: an array of individual entities that have, through multiple and varied experiences, grown in all possible directions.

Speed of Movement

The second concept in regards to evolution is the increasing speed of movement. As before, when discussing the concept of expansion we will look at the increasing speed of movement as a concept, before addressing the idea we are familiar with that faster is not necessarily better. Firstly though we shall look at the idea of movement, without which we could not discuss the concept of the increasing speed of movement.

Every individual entity requires either an internal or external force to generate movement. If an entity existed that consisted of no internal movement, then it would need an external moving force to interact with to generate movement. This would then seem to suggest that the generation of any movement must have needed a prior movement (force) of some kind.

The issue here is that it is impossible for there to be a first cause of movement, as movement can only occur when movement already exists. Therefore the concept of movement, such as the concepts of infinity (∞) and absolute zero (0), exists in definition to its opposite. The concept of stagnation or absolute stillness is defined by the concept of movement. Although more precisely it is the concept of infinite speed that defines the concept of absolute stillness. These two concepts are akin to pure nothingness and Infinitum Perfectus, as they represent absence and perfection (in terms of speed). Of course like the concepts of pure nothingness and Infinitum Perfectus the concepts of infinite speed and absolute stillness are unobservable in their actuality. Only the idea (or misconception) of absolute stillness and infinite speed is ever actually observed.

Additionally we also have the concept of the fastest speed of movement defined by the concept of the slowest speed of movement. These concepts, along with every possible speed of movement, exist within the concepts of infinite speed and absolute stillness. One of the reasons these concepts are different to the concepts of infinite speed and absolute stillness is that the fastest speed of movement and the slowest speed of movement neither represent perfection nor an absence. The same applies to the concepts of the biggest and the smallest, along with the longest and the shortest, and other similar concepts involving measurements. The difference between the slowest and the fastest, or even the biggest and the smallest, compared with something that is infinite, is that they are a (temporary) fixed point. Something that represents an absence, such as absolute stillness or 0, is not a fixed point as it is merely a void. Something that is infinite, or a representation of perfection is never a fixed point as it is truly endless; remembering that perfection is also an endless journey. Even though in actuality our idea of what the smallest, biggest, slowest or fastest entity is will likely change, the concepts themselves represent a fixed point.

To make this easier to understand we will once again look at mathematics, specifically the concepts of the highest and lowest number. The lowest number is not 0 as it is really an absence of a number, while ∞ is not a representation of the highest number, or a number at all for that matter, as it rather represents the endless amount of numbers in mathematics. The concept of the highest number would have to represent a single number, even though in actuality there would be no set number, as it is with the lowest number (remembering that 1 is not the actual lowest number thanks to the decimal system). This is because the highest and lowest number would always be open to change for each individual, but the concepts themselves will always represent a fixed number (point). All concepts involving measurements, such as the biggest and the smallest or the fastest and the slowest, follow this same logic.

The distinction between the fastest speed and infinite speed may be hard to grasp and in relation to other ideas in the book it is slightly less important. If these ideas regarding speed are hard to make sense of it may be easier just to think of it as: all possible speeds of movement defining and being defined by the idea of stagnation.

Constant Changes in Speed

Following the pattern of previously discussed concepts, the reason why any speed of movement within any entity gets faster (or slower) is its juxtaposition to other speeds of movement. Once again this may seem like an overly simplistic answer, but it is in fact the only possible explanation. There are two main points that need to be taken into consideration for this idea to make sense.

If all speed of movement was at any point the same then nothing could increase or decrease in speed. There would be no differing force to affect the speed of movement of other entities. Therefore to account for all the various speeds of movement that we as humans can currently identify, those differing speeds of movement would had to have always existed. The same would logically apply to speeds of movement we have yet to encounter.

Nothing becomes faster or slower randomly; it is always influenced by an external source. Even in our known physical world there needs to be an external influence to cause something to move faster or slower.

This then leads to the second point, which is that no two entities can literally have the same speed of movement. For any two entities to have the exact same speed of movement the two entities would in fact have to be exactly the same; in other words having the exact same experiences. As every entity is literally different in some way due to their own unique experiences, their internal movements will also be different. One may think that surely at some point there would have been two entities with the exact same speed of movement. This idea would, however, be forgetting the law of infinity. On ever-closer examination, no matter how similar two entities are, there will eventually be differences found, including in their speed of movement.

Therefore as every entity must contain a unique speed of movement, along with the fact that there are an infinite number of entities in existence, then there will literally be an infinite number of speeds of movement. This of course reiterates the fact that there can be no literal fastest or slowest speed of movement in actuality. It also means that every entity's speed of movement will in fact be constantly changing, as they will be forever influenced and defined by differing speeds of movement from an infinite number of external entities.

If not already, the reason why speed of movement and for that matter size are important to evolution, rather than merely acting as arbitrary differences between entities, will ironically be made clearer in the next section: *When Bigger and Faster Are Not Better*.

Positive and Negative Influences

Before addressing the concepts of size and speed further there is one more aspect of evolution we want to address. Although Infinitum Perfectus exists due to its juxtaposition to pure nothingness, which could be considered an absolute negative, evolution itself is not merely based upon a reaction to something negative. Even if we focus on our known world there are those individuals that inspire others to do good and improve themselves in some fashion. These people would usually be simultaneously repulsed to some degree by negative behavior and attracted to those that exhibit positive behavior. As infinity is truly endless, along with the fact that neither complete perfection nor imperfection can become actualities, there will always be entities that are either more advanced or less advanced for any individual to react against. There will literally be an infinite number of more advanced individuals to inspire evolutionary progress, while there will also be an infinite number of less advanced individuals to be repulsed by. For individuals that regress the opposite of course applies.

Even if an individual does not subjectively appear to be in the direct vicinity of another individual that is either less or more advanced, the concept of Infinitum Perfectus (allowing for increasing perfection) and pure nothingness (allowing for increasing imperfection) will always be true. Therefore the influencing factors of evolution and regression will always have effect, even if they cannot be subjectively observed or consciously understood.

When Bigger and Faster Are Not Better

When Bigger Appears Not to Be Better

Sometimes in our everyday lives we will come across situations or observe something that suggests that bigger is not necessarily better. Quite often it could be argued that bigger is in fact worse than something that is smaller. We will look at several examples in order to better make sense of this. The first example we will look at is the size of animals. The biggest creature to live on Earth, the blue whale, and the current biggest land mammal, the elephant, will be the prime examples. One thing about these animals is that their size and strength make them formidable targets for predators, as opposed to smaller, less bulky animals. They also have more fat (energy stores) than other animals, which is another positive. Paradoxically they also need more physical sustenance to survive, making their size problematic if there was a long-term food shortage. Other problems with larger animals is their lack of maneuverability compared to much smaller, nimble animals, which can hide in small spaces and avoid hunters (usually humans) or natural disasters.

Now the important thing to consider here is the physical size of an elephant or a blue whale corresponds to their greater physical strength relative to other animals, including humans. However, their physical size does not make them the most intelligent or most flexible entities on Earth. Therefore the biggest animals on Earth are not necessary the most evolved. A bigger brain, or more specifically the largest amount of used brain matter, leads to the chance of greater intelligence; although this of course depends on other factors such as emotions.

An animal, a building or anything you can think of has various qualities that make up their value. The tallest building may be greater than other buildings if you only take into account its storage capacity or economy of space, but that does not mean that it will be the most stable building. The building with the biggest and strongest base, such as a pyramid, will be far more stable than a skyscraper. Of course the pyramid is seen as less practical this day and age, due to the large amount of ground its base requires for its corresponding storage capacity.

What buildings and living beings alike require to genuinely improve (evolve) is a sense of balance; or to put it another way, a balanced way of growing. If a living entity grows in terms of: strength (not only physical but emotional), intelligence (including memory capacity), flexibility, ego (not to be confused with the inflated ego), sensitivity in terms of perception and any other quality, then this would be considered the best form of growth. It's not literally possible to grow in all of these areas to the exact same degree, but the closest an individual can come to growing in a perfectly balanced way, the better their evolutionary progress will be. Therefore when all aspects of either a single entity or the whole of existence grow in (almost) unison, then and only then can one really say that bigger is better.

When Faster Appears Not to Be Better

Like the notion of 'bigger is better' the idea that faster is better does not always ring true in our everyday lives. The faster someone drives their car then the less control they are likely to have in regards to maneuvering effectively through windy roads, avoiding obstacles, or coming to a complete stop. The same can be said for an animal or human that is running too fast; they will inevitably have less control when it comes to maneuverability or having to stop suddenly. This can also apply to the workplace, where doing any type of job too fast, whether physical, mental or both, can lead to errors and an inferior performance.

There is, however, no set speed that all individuals should operate at. The important aspect to an individual's speed of movement in terms of evolutionary progression is that every speed of movement within that individual needs to be as balanced as possible. If someone's arm movement in performing a chore is faster in relation to their ability to react to external influences, then there is a higher chance for errors to occur compared to a more balanced individual. However, if someone's calculating abilities matched the fastest rate at which they could physically move, then the faster that individual could perform physical tasks effectively. For instance in regards to driving a car, the faster someone's reaction time, the faster they can adequately react to changing external situations. Therefore the faster they are able to drive a car safely.

This principle works in all situations. Every aspect of a person, or any entity, needs to become faster in a relatively equal and balanced way for the concept of 'faster is better' to be true. Even if one aspect of an individual is noticeably slower than all other aspects then that individual will still be unbalanced and the concept of 'faster is better' will not always be true for that individual. Therefore speed like size must increase at almost the same rate in regards to every aspect of an individual for true evolutionary progress to occur.

Interaction

Another aspect of the fluid existence we are all a part of, and a major factor of evolution, is interaction. If nothing were to interact, thereby causing a reaction, then evolution would not exist, as nothing would be stimulated into change of any kind. From our subjective human perspective interaction can be broken down into two distinct types: internal and external interaction.

External and Internal Interactions

If we used humans as a model to explain the two types of interaction, we can see that neither type of interaction can occur without the other. External interactions are of course any external influence that can affect an individual, whether it is in the form of: nonphysical interaction, such as conversing with another person, or physical interaction, such as being touched by another entity.

Internal interactions could be thought of as, for instance, the different parts of the human brain communicating information to itself, which was received from an external interaction. For example when someone talks to you (external interaction) you then interpret what they say in your mind (internal interaction), which will then likely stimulate further external interactions, and so the cycle goes. Internal interactions are not only done to communicate external information throughout the rest of the body, they are also obviously needed to keep the body functioning (properly or otherwise).

In actuality all interactions should be thought of as the same in principle. Whether something appears as an internal or external interaction depends on the individual's subjective notion of what is and isn't an individual. Internal interactions could be thought of as what occurs within a universe, an individual human, a single cell of an organism and so on. The same applies to external interactions, whereby anything that is subjectively thought of as an individual can affect anything else that is subjectively thought of as an individual.

Subjective Interactions

When and if an interaction occurs is also subjective. Whether someone reacts to someone's verbal or physical gestures as a form of communication is subjective in terms of not only comprehension, but of awareness. Whether direct physical interaction actually occurs, in other words what we would think of as the direct contact between two entities, is also subjective.

When we shake someone's hand we are likely to think that we are physically interacting with that person. In actuality there is something in between the two shaking hands, which in this instance could be seen as compressed particles from the atmosphere, depending on how closely we observe the handshake. If we could zoom in indefinitely upon a handshake, we would not only see less of a connection between the two hands, but we would see different entities (atoms, subatomic particles, etc) appearing to connect or disconnect at different stages. Eventually we might not see a connection between what we believe are the two individual hands at all.

Although from our subjective point of view, unaided by technology, a handshake is a clear interaction between two individual people. From other nonhuman perspectives the interaction of much smaller entities, some of which may not appear connected to either hand, is either also occurring, or is in fact the only interaction occurring.

Any interaction anywhere in the whole of existence will always be subjective, no matter how definite it might appear to our limited perspectives. Of course two-way interaction occurs when both parties subjectively believe they are interacting. The more similar the two entities are that are interacting the stronger the connection will be. The important thing to take from this is that the belief that interaction is occurring is enough to allow for evolutionary change, which subsequently allows for the eternal journey to perfection.

The Concept of Attraction

The concept of interaction must also take into account the concept of attraction, as inevitably any interaction will involve either some form of attraction or repulsion. In nature, including chemistry, biology, physics and simple human behavior, there are instances of attraction and repulsion, which play out a necessary component of how existence and growth operate.

There are of course instances where similar entities and forces attract one another, while simultaneously repelled by their (subjective) opposites. This then allows for both the concepts of growth/evolution and subjective individualism. Additionally, in some instances, opposites are also attracted to one another to some degree. In actuality to allow for perpetual evolution the ideas of opposites attracting one another, and that which is similar attracting each other, occurs constantly and side by side.

As discussed previously for any entity to exist that which is similar must attract each other in order to get a whole, recognizable individual. If similar entities all repelled each other, then nothing would grow or take form, making existence itself completely unfathomable. Therefore the idea of opposites attracting one another could seem counterintuitive. The fact is that the attraction of opposites is what creates something that is new. The concepts of pure nothingness and Infinitum Perfectus juxtaposed to one another has allowed for, not only existence itself, but also the infinite number of unique entities within existence. To allow for evolution, the driving law of all existence, then opposites must be juxtaposed to one another, either metaphorically in the form of ideas, or physically. To put simply, for something to perfect itself it must be aware of its 'opposites' in order to continually refine itself. Opposites may not be attracted to each other to such an extent that they form subjective wholes, but the attraction is strong enough to create an intimate awareness of one another.

Humans are one example of entities that can be attracted to either their subjective opposites or those that are similar. In most cases humans are likely to be attracted to someone that exhibits characteristics that are both similar and dissimilar. They can be attracted to someone that is very similar in order to feel a certain oneness, but simultaneously there can also be differences that can either help an individual refine oneself, or lead to regression. For example a violent partner could help strengthen an individual's self in a moral sense by being repelled by such behavior, while fortifying their own self-worth. On the other hand they can become defeated with a lowering of their self-esteem and inwardly regress.

Obviously what any individual entity considers to be similar to itself or the opposite of itself is subjective. The important thing here is that individuals react in a way which suggests that they believe that they are similar or dissimilar to any other individual. This applies to what we would subjectively consider to be the least evolved to the most evolved entities. It is in fact what the individual believes about other individuals that is important in regards to how they react, whether such similarities are based upon: emotions, intellect, physicality or in any way beyond our current comprehension.

Attraction and False Evolution

The attraction of opposites can also lead to the idea of false evolution. This can be seen at work most notably in humans when an individual is attracted to what at least appears to be their opposite in one or more specific areas. For example this could be seen if one individual wanted to couple with another that had superior self-confidence, as they wished to (consciously or subconsciously) incorporate this attribute within themselves.

If they have within themselves a high potential for self-confidence then this attribute may awaken within them, but if not the opposite effect may occur. In opposition to their partner's superior self-confidence they may regress further rather than evolve; effectively becoming the 'opposite' of their partner in regards to self-confidence. This simply occurs as their lack of self-confidence is more and more defined in opposition to their partner's superior self-confidence. This works in the same way that the concepts of black and white or pure nothingness and Infinitum Perfectus define each other as complete opposites. Either the individual will become inspired in terms of growing their self-confidence, or they will regress, as true stagnation is not literally possible.

If the individual with the poor self-confidence is consciously aware of their problem they can, in opposition to this short-coming, seek to overcome this issue in a more natural way. One could surmise that if this individual is choosing the 'fast and easy' way to gain greater self-confidence by choosing a partner with these qualities, then they are less likely to actually build these qualities naturally.

This particular situation would depend on the motivation of the individual. They may either want someone to help inspire them develop these qualities, or they may just want these qualities in their life without having to develop them naturally. If the latter is the case then this can be thought of as false evolution, as true evolution within the individual is not actually occurring. This is only one example of false evolution, but any human example of false evolution would follow a similar pattern.

Chapter 3

Good and Evil – Right and Wrong

Defining Good and Evil

The previous chapter dealt largely with the concept of evolution, with a focus on the idea of growth. Most of this focused on what we might consider the physical (or metaphysical if one prefers) idea of growing in size and speed. Aside from a very brief look at 'false evolution' the chapter did not address the outcomes of improvement. This is whereby an individual that has grown in a fairly balanced fashion would exhibit traits that could be considered 'good' in comparison to an individual that has grown either: unevenly, at a slower rate, or in fact had regressed rather than grown. There could then be a distinction of 'good' and 'evil' between an individual that has grown in a fairly even fashion (becoming good) compared to an individual that has, on the whole, regressed (becoming evil).

The term 'evil' has a certain religious (although the nonreligious can also use this term) connotation that may cloud the reader's idea of what we are trying to address. If the 'absolute good' can be thought of as doing the best possible thing in any given situation, then 'absolute evil' is doing the worst possible thing in any given situation. The various levels of good and evil would of course exist in between these two absolutes.

This is a rather simplistic description of good and evil, and to work in the everyday world it would have to be put into some kind of context. Additionally good and evil can be thought of as subjective and therefore perhaps meaningless. One person may appear 'good' compared to one particular person, while simultaneously appearing 'evil' in comparison with another. If we define the 'absolute good' and 'absolute evil' as *basic concepts that underpin existence* then they can have a more objective meaning associated with evolutionary growth.

Absolute Good and Evil or Better and Worse?

Although the term 'absolute evil' is often used in society to describe something we consider heinous, it is not technically used in an appropriate way. It is being used in a subjective way rather than to describe anything that is an absolute. The frequent use of this term may be due to the human desire to see things in black and white, as it is easier than dealing with the infinite shades of grey.

Much like the concepts of 0 and ∞, the concepts of the absolute good and absolute evil are true in theory but will never actually be perceived by any individual. We could in fact think of absolute evil (complete imperfection) as pure nothingness and the absolute good (perfection) as Infinitum Perfectus. As the world we are familiar with appears to be an ongoing process it may be better, at least in our everyday lives, to think in terms of 'better' and 'worse', rather than the absolute good and absolute evil. To better illustrate why, we will look at examples that can affect the modern world we live in. Several of these examples may seem emotionally unappealing, but are technically accurate, so the reader should keep this is mind when reading further.

Examples of Better and Worse

If a megalomaniacal state leader ordered the death of 3 million people it may at first seem to be an act of absolute evil. If this were true then the death of 4 million people would also have to be considered an act of absolute evil, as there is nothing more evil than the idea of absolute evil. This is despite the fact that 1 million more people have died. Obviously the law of infinity would, as previously mentioned, relegate the idea of absolute evil to the realm of concepts and subjectivity. This is because no matter how evil a deed was there could always be a deed that was even more evil. Even if we were to use labels that were not considered absolutes, such as extremely evil, very evil or just plain 'evil', a similar issue will arise.

There would need to be a line drawn to suggest what was extremely evil as opposed to very evil and plain 'evil'. If 100,000 killings were considered very evil and 3 million extremely evil, the change from going to very to extremely evil is not going to be a set number. It would always be a subjective number, most likely based upon an emotional reaction. This is where the terms 'better' and 'worse' can be used far more effectively. Technically 3 million killings is worse than the killing of 100,000 people, and 4 million worse than 3 million. Although it may sound abhorrent, 100,000 killings is technically better than 3 million killings as the notion of 'better' is the direct opposite of 'worse'.

To determine what is better or worse in regards to the killing of others, we must consider more than just simply the number of killings. The motives of killing someone also needs to be taken into account. Killing one individual to save 100,000 could be considered by many as a better choice than not killing that individual, assuming there was no other way to prevent those 100,000 deaths. There are of course various scenarios that we could conceive of where killing an individual or a few individuals could appear a better overall choice than not killing those individuals. Although to truly know this we would need all the specifics of the situation, which is often hard to do.

If we continue with the idea of humans killing other humans, as it is arguably one of the most contentious human behaviors, we should look at this behavior in terms of evolution. The evolution we are looking at is based more upon individual consciousness and society, rather than any form of physical change alone. To do this we will compare two examples.

The first is a tribal man living thousands of years ago who kills an intruder intent on murder and stealing his tribe's food. The primary motivation of the tribal man was to protect his own life and prolong his family/tribal line. In other words the motivation for killing the intruder is based on the idea of physical survival.

The other example is of a contemporary man who has killed someone that he has never met. He has committed this murder to, at least temporarily, alleviate his own insecurity and emotional weakness. This was done by exercising physical power over another; in other words murdering someone in order to generate a sense of self-worth. This could be seen as, rather than killing someone to protect his own physical life, a way of protecting his sense of what his ego (self-worth) should be. This is fundamentally done by disempowering another individual, so that he can then feel superior in contrast to his murder victim.

Both of these men have killed another individual due to a sense of insecurity. The tribal man is insecure about his physical life and that of his family/tribe. The contemporary man is insecure about his own fragile ego. The tribal man's actions were based upon the physical fragility of the human body, which needs protecting in a physical way. In basic terms the dog eat dog world of a few thousand years ago was based around survival of the physically fittest to some degree. Therefore the tribal man has proven himself stronger, whether by individual strength or utilizing the strength of the whole tribe to defeat the intruder. The tribal man has then allowed for both his and his tribe's evolutionary progress to continue.

If by learning that a better defense of the tribe is needed, in the form of developing a fortified stronghold (simultaneously lessening the need to kill others to protect themselves), the tribe will have evolved as a small society. If the tribe continually sees killing others as the only way to protect themselves from outsiders, then the tribe's evolutionary progress will gradually falter. They will be seen as a threat by other tribes that are willing to cooperate with one another, and they will eventually become ostracized.

The contemporary man's actions are based upon a mixture of

mental and emotional issues that need repairing on a mental and emotional level, rather than attempting to weaken others in order to empower himself. This attempt to lower the stature of others is in fact another example of false evolutionary progression. It merely inflates the ego artificially, and most likely blocks any sense of nonphysical evolution.

Even though these examples may seem obvious to us as to what is better and worse, there will always be examples that are hard to determine either way due to the limitations of our perceptive abilities. There will still be a subjective element when assessing certain situations and actions. For actual evolution to occur, which is required for the concept of Infinitum Perfectus to exist, the ideas of 'better' and 'worse' by themselves can be limited. For evolution to be an actuality there also needs to be the concept of 'objective evolution'.

Objective Evolution

From the human point of view it might be hard to imagine what actions actually lead to objectively evolving or objectively regressing. Our individual situations are always different, and what we can compare with our own reactions and ideas is usually limited. Usually the best we can do is examine our options and consider what options seem worse and which ones seem better.

Does the Notion of 'Better' Always Mean Objectively Evolving?

There is, however, an issue in regards to merely comparing a limited number of options or 'things' with one another in order to determine which is better. To illustrate this issue we will look at the example of two boys reacting differently when they learn that their girlfriend wants to break up with them. One boy chooses to physically abuse his girlfriend, while the other verbally abuses her without physically harming her. If we had to choose between the two most of us would likely consider the choice to verbally abuse the girlfriend as 'better' than physically abusing her. The obvious issue here is that labeling a specific action as 'better' compared to one other action is not always going to lead to the path of objective evolution. Objective evolution transcends what we subjectively consider to be better and worse, as often what we considered to be better (in comparison to something else) is still actually objectively regressing.

For some very basic individuals the choice to verbally abuse their girlfriend, rather than physically abusing her, may in fact be a form of progression, therefore they have objectively evolved. Even though verbally abusing someone would be abhorrent to many of us, for someone that has only ever used physical violence in dealing with issues this could only be thought of as progression. For many of us the use of either physical or verbal abuse would most likely be an action that led to objectively regressing, rather than objectively evolving. Therefore another option would be required. That third option may not be straight-forward either. It would depend on the evolutionary progress of the individual. In any situation there would in fact be various options for a particular individual that would be considered objectively evolving, and simultaneously various options that would be considered objectively regressing.

Although the example regarding the abusive boyfriend may have been obvious due to its extreme nature, every reaction that a human commits will in fact fall under the concept of either objectively evolving or objectively regressing. As true stagnation is not possible every entity will either be evolving or regressing for every given reaction that they have. However, it is likely to be an infrequent occurrence to notice either evolution or regression within one's own self, or within anyone else for that matter.

Assessing Good and Evil in Terms of Objectively Evolving

There are a number of reasons why it is hard to know whether we are objectively evolving or not. Many of the smaller reactions we have would be quite difficult if not close to impossible to assess in terms of objective evolution. This is once again due to our limited abilities of perception. This is especially true for what we may consider to be seemingly uncontentious decisions. For example being able to run faster for a human would be considered evolving as a professional runner, but would it be considered as evolving on the whole?

There would be subjective answers to this obviously, but also an objective answer, depending on the specifics. Basically it would depend on whether or not being able to run faster improved the individual as a whole. For instance if it actually detracted from other areas of the individual, subsequently impeding the individual's evolution on the whole, then being able to run faster would not lead to objectively evolving. Objectively evolving of course needs to take into consideration every aspect of an individual entity, and not merely one or two aspects. An individual that evolves in regards to two specific abilities, while regressing to the same degree in regards to four other abilities, would still not be objectively evolving.

In any given situation requiring a reaction of any kind there is a theoretical 'best option' and a theoretical 'worst option'. In between these two options are of course the ideas of better and worse, but also the concepts of objectively good and objectively bad (evil). This is where any option that was objectively good would lead to objectively evolving, while an objectively bad option would lead to objectively regressing. Subjectively good on the other hand would be a limited assessment of an idea or reaction due to our limited knowledge and experience. This is not to say that what is considered to be subjectively good is not also objectively evolving, but the degree of 'good' or 'bad' itself could not be completely accurate.

Although this could all sound confusing, the important thing to know is that in reality every reaction an entity has will either lead to objectively evolving or objectively regressing. In other words there is an invisible line drawn between the infinite number of reactions one can have to any given circumstance. That which is objectively bad (objectively regressing) on one side, and that which is objectively good (objectively evolving) on the other. However, as we are limited to viewing our lives in a subjective rather than objective fashion, we can only experience a world of 'better' and 'worse'.

How to Achieve the Best Possible Outcome

Even though the 'best' or 'worst' possible reaction in any given situation exists in theory, it would be literally impossible for any individual to achieve this feat. To do so an individual would need all possible information regarding the situation, which would literally involve knowledge of all existence. This is due to the notion that every action/reaction leads to an infinite number of subsequent reactions, which will eventually have some kind of effect on the whole of existence. Even though such effects could subjectively seem extremely minute and would obviously appear far from instantaneous, those effects are real nonetheless. To literally know everything about existence the individual would have to be themselves perfect; and as discussed previously, this is not possible. In other words to react perfectly or make a perfect decision, one's capabilities and knowledge would also have to be perfect.

Therefore, even though the concepts of what is objectively best and what is objectively worst are true, we as individuals will only ever experience that which is objectively good or objectively worse. Even though we cannot always know what is objectively good or objectively worse in any given situation, because as previously mentioned we live in a subjective world of 'better' and 'worse', it will still nevertheless have an actual effect on us. When and how an individual notices the effects of their own behavior and whether they are objectively evolving or not will depend on how evolved that individual is.

The main point that we all need to remember is that without the concept of objective evolution being true (the simple idea of becoming better rather than worse) all of existence could not be. If objective evolution did not exist there could only ever be randomness or pure nothingness, making the concept of Infinitum Perfectus untenable. As Infinitum Perfectus, the concept of a perfectly evolved existence, is defined by and defines pure nothingness, then the concept of objective evolution, even if we cannot observe this in a completely accurate way, must be true. You cannot have the concept of Infinitum Perfectus, which incorporates the process of existence eternally perfecting itself, without the concept of objective evolution, along with its defining opposite, objective regression.

Knowledge and Objectivity: Right and Wrong

In regards to knowledge the ideas of 'good' and 'evil/bad' also apply, albeit with less emotional attachment than the examples in the previous section, which most people would categorize as moral issues. Before looking more closely at the ideas of right and wrong, we will briefly address their connection with good and evil. The reason is that some may view the idea of evil and being wrong, or more specifically making an unintentional mistake, as completely separate.

Evil: A Mere Mistake?

At first one might not see any correlation with making a simple mistake, such as a mathematical error, with the idea of evil. A mathematical error would usually be considered as 'wrong' or a 'mistake', rather than 'evil', while accidents are also usually considered as 'mistakes'. On the other hand deliberate actions that cause harm, most often carried out by a perpetrator towards other individuals are thought of as being 'evil' rather than being a mistake.

We usually consider such deliberate actions of 'evil' to be reserved for humans with their higher levels of consciousness compared to that of animals and other less evolved entities. The question of whether animals or less evolved entities can commit deliberate acts of 'evil' could take a whole chapter in itself. Therefore this specific question won't be addressed here.

In reality any reaction or thought that could be considered truly evil is, at its fundamental essence, a mistake. The main reason that a human's deliberate act of harm (or evil) is actually a mistake is that it is in fact an attempt to solve insecurities in the fastest, and usually laziest, way possible. This subsequently impedes natural evolution. We can look at the examples of killing and stealing to make this clearer.

Stealing rather than earning creates distrust within society and works towards isolating the individual that steals. This then limits that individual's evolution due to decreasing the chance for varied challenges which aid evolution. Killing in order to steal of course would have a similar if not more severe result, while killing someone to alleviate one's personal insecurities, as discussed earlier in the chapter, is a false effort to evolve. Therefore the mistake is that these actions that are considered 'evil' usually lead to regression rather than evolution, with the individual themselves most likely completely unaware of this. Any actions that lead to regression, no matter how immoral we subjectively consider these actions to be, are merely born from making mistakes.

Perfecting Knowledge

Obviously to better avoid making mistakes any individual needs sufficient knowledge to make better, rather than worse decisions in their life/existence. Knowledge may seem like something that should only fall into an objective category; either something is wrong or it is right. If someone were to say that: 'an orange is a citrus fruit and not a vegetable' then, in our current context, this statement would be considered right and not wrong. Technically there are elements of both vegetables and citrus fruits that are the same, but from our human perspective an orange appears to have more in common with other citrus fruits than it does with vegetables. When an individual's knowledge improves such a statement may improve slightly to say something more along the lines of: 'an orange has more in common with other citrus fruits than it does with vegetables'. When the individual's knowledge improves even further, such statements will become even more specific.

The point we are trying to make is that knowledge goes from a broad understanding to a more and more specific under-standing of any given topic. For instance human knowledge about trees has evolved over the years, along with rest of nature and the universe. At some stage humanity may have seen trees as a source of food in the form of fruit and nuts. Later on in human development trees would have also been seen as a source of building materials in the form of wood, and then more recently as a source of oxygen through the process of photosyn-thesis. Therefore knowledge on the majority of subjects should be thought of as continually perfecting itself, rather than ever being absolutely right or absolutely wrong. We will soon discuss what types of knowledge can be truly thought of as absolutely right or absolutely wrong in the subsection: *Objective Truth*.

Transition From Right to Wrong

Despite this view that the majority of knowledge will never be completely perfect, there will still be a point when an idea begins to be objectively more right than wrong. Although we would be unable to see it, there will be an objective line separating all the conceivable ideas about any given topic in our actual existence. On one side will be the ideas that are more right than wrong, and on the other the ideas that are more wrong than right. Although it may seem strange at first, every conceivable idea about any given topic in our actual existence could be objectively ranked in terms of how 'right' or 'wrong' they were. In other words when comparing two ideas about any topic that are both objectively more right than wrong, there will always be an idea that is objectively more right than the other. The same of course applies to ideas that are more wrong than right. To make more sense of this we will look at two examples involving oranges.

In our current society the statement: 'an orange is a fruit' and the statement: 'an orange is an object', would both be considered right. Even if both of these statements are objectively more right than wrong, one of these statements will still be objectively more right than the other. With our current knowledge of oranges we should feel safe in thinking that the first statement is objectively more right than the second, as it is far more specific. Sometimes of course it is not so easy to make such an assessment.

If someone said that: 'an orange was a rock', while someone else said that: 'an orange was a seagull', most (relatively sane) people would consider both of these statements to be wrong. Although most people might consider these statements to be equally wrong, objectively one idea must be more wrong than the other. The more knowledge an individual has in regards to oranges, seagulls and rocks, the more accurate their assessment can be. Objectively either a rock or a seagull is closer to being an orange than the other, in as much as they have a greater number of similar elements and characteristics to an orange. Regardless of how dissimilar these three things are to each other from our subjective viewpoint, they will always contain similar elements that make up their composition. Therefore, objectively no two ideas about any given topic in our actual existence can be as equally wrong, or as equally right as each other. However, both ideas could still be objectively more right than wrong, or vice versa.

The more knowledge an individual has about a topic in our actual existence the more accurate they can be in assessing how right or wrong ideas are in relation to that topic. No individual entity can know absolutely everything about anything that constantly changes (evolving and regressing) and consists of an infinite amount of detail. Therefore only that which does not change can be talked about in terms of what is absolutely right and wrong, which inevitably refers to nonhuman created concepts. This is not to be confused with concepts that have merely been labeled via a human language. These concepts, such as the *basic concepts that underpin existence*, are the only knowledge that should be called objectively truths.

Objective Truth

Knowledge that is objectively true, rather than objectively more right than wrong, must be eternally unchanging and complete in all necessary detail. This is where no other detail is needed as the idea is already completely accurate. Any *basic concept that underpins existence* should be considered an objective truth, as they are eternal, unchanging, and if represented (written) correctly complete in all necessary detail. If someone came to the wrong conclusion in regards to a *basic concept that underpins existence*, then their fundamental idea of existence would be skewed, leading that person to further misconceptions. This would occur even if the conclusion was only slightly wrong.

The basic equation of $1 + 1 = 2$ is a good example of an eternal concept that contains all the necessary detail to be absolutely true. No further information is needed to add to this equation's basic truth. Stating that $1 + 1 = 2$ because it does not equal 3 or any other number does not actually make this mathematical concept any more accurate than the more simple equation of $1 + 1 = 2$. The added information, although not untrue, is superfluous and does not make the concept any more true because of the added information. Saying that $7 \times 7 = 49$, but almost equals

50 is not only superfluous, but it is also subjective, as the idea of what 'almost' is would have a different meaning to different individuals. Only the concept of 7 x 7 = 49 is an objective truth, and no amount of extra information could make it any more true than it already is.

To say that 1 + 1 = 3 is less incorrect than 1 + 1 = 4 is technically true, as it is literally closer, but they must both be considered incorrect, as an objective truth can only have one correct answer. Therefore in relation to objective truths you can have one correct answer, or an infinite number of increasingly incorrect answers. There is also no least incorrect answer. To make sense of this we will look at another equation. To say that 1 + 1 = 2.00001 is of course not the least incorrect answer. The reason is perhaps obvious upon looking at the equation, as there could be an infinite number of zeroes placed in between the 2 and the .01. This principle is true for all concepts, due to the law of infinity.

In regards to the *basic concepts that underpin existence* there can in fact be the 'most incorrect' answer. This can only be done when dealing with complete opposites. To say that 0 equaled ∞ or that black equaled white would be considered the most incorrect answer; in other words you could not conceivably get further away from the objective truth. To say that the concept of black equaled the concept of ∞ is not, however, the most incorrect answer. The concept of color or light and the concept of mathematics, although stemming from the same source, are in fact separate concepts. Therefore this idea would become a metaphor that could be subjectively interpreted in various ways. Only equating two exact opposites in terms of concepts can be the 'most incorrect'.

An answer that is not objectively true in regards to any *basic concept that underpins existence* has been made for either two reasons. One is that they were deliberately wrong for whatever reason or, most likely, they were incapable of knowing the right answer as they had insufficient knowledge to understand the concept in question.

Are Concepts Latent Knowledge?

If insufficient knowledge causes the inability to recognize *basic concepts that underpin existence*, then obviously sufficient knowledge enables their recognition. The question would then be: where does this knowledge come from? Do individuals inherently know (subconsciously) basic concepts that are objective truths or do they need to be discovered through experience? As all entities are a part of existence, one might think that they should inherently have the appropriate information, but this does not seem like the case. For humans there is an increasing awareness of these concepts as we go through our various life experiences.

Whether or not these concepts are discovered internally like a form of dormant knowledge, or whether they need to be discovered externally, it is the process of observing the known world that makes us conscious of these concepts. More specifically it is the act of contemplation and the ability to both recognize repeating patterns and conceptualize complex ideas derived from external influences that allow for the recognition of concepts.

This would suggest that only entities with enough imagination to be able to conceptualize, and the ability to consciously contemplate are able to understand the *basic concepts that underpin existence*. The truth is, a basic recognition of these concepts does not necessarily need a human (or higher) level of consciousness. It might be hard at first to consider that a plant could be aware of any *basic concepts that underpin existence*. As plants do not have the brain or nervous system associated with animals or humans they most likely cannot contemplate or have complex imaginations. Plants are, however, aware of light and react favorably to certain amounts of light. These reactions are of course not the type of conscious decisions that we are familiar with. They would rather be deemed as chemical reactions brought about by external influences.

The fact is that the brain activity leading to human thoughts are also chemical reactions that are derived from external influences, albeit more complex than the reactions of a plant. Humans can react to memories or ideas that are not immediately affecting them from external influences, but those ideas and memories were originally derived from external sources. If a human's thoughts are internal reactions, derived from interactions with external sources, then understanding a *basic concept that underpins existence* will be a form of reaction to that concept. Therefore an individual entity's differing reaction (including a plant) to light and dark is at least some form of 'understanding' or, perhaps more appropriately, a recognition of those concepts. However, this is not to suggest that a plant understands light and dark in the same way as humans do, or is able to react in the same way as humans do in the face of other concepts.

An individual entity's level of complexity appears to determine how they understand and react to any concept. As our internal reactions are complex enough to allow for contemplation, rather than just reactions to immediate external influences, humans are (most likely) able to comprehend far more basic concepts than plants. If the ability to recognize the *basic concepts that underpin existence* works as everything else in the evolutionary process, such as human knowledge, then the greater an individual's intelligence becomes, the greater their understanding of such concepts will be.

Knowing Every Concept

Someone may say that when an individual completely understands the concept of $1 + 1 = 2$, it cannot be better understood and therefore the understanding of this concept is perfect. This is despite the fact that a seemingly imperfect individual has understood this concept. This would surely suggest that before perfection is reached by an individual, every single conceivable concept that underpins existence will be known and understood perfectly. Therefore it might seem contradictory that an individual could understand the complete workings of existence and yet never themselves reach perfection due to the laws of infinity.

There are two points to consider. The concept of $1 + 1 = 2$ is merely one minute part of the much more overly complicated and overarching concept of mathematics. The other point is that this concept is also only one part of one overarching concept among many other overarching concepts. Within each overarching concept there are an infinite number of individual concepts. In other words no matter how far our knowledge advances there would still be an infinite number of concepts left to understand.

Most of these concepts would currently be beyond our comprehension, but they would still be offshoots of the basic concepts we have discussed in this book. In other words there are always increasingly more specific concepts that make up much broader concepts, much in the way that growth in terms of size and speed falls under the basic concept of evolution. This will be discussed a little further in the final chapter: *Tiers*, which briefly looks at the different tiers that these concepts fall under. When an individual evolves they will continually recognize further concepts as objective truths, without being able to recognize and understand every possible concept until perfection has been (theoretically) reached. Just like knowing everything possible about the cosmos and how it works, knowledge about every conceivable concept that underpins existence will infinitely improve without ever being complete.

Chapter 4

Existing Misconceptions

There are of course many misconceptions that humans have about their reality, as their knowledge and perceptive abilities are far from perfect. As perfection is not an actual possibility, every individual entity in existence will always have some form of misconception about existence. The common misconceptions discussed here: randomness and time, are important to address as they can affect the way an individual thinks about the whole of existence.

Randomness

As Infinitum Perfectus is defined by the concept of pure nothingness, which in turn sees all of existence as an eternal journey towards perfection, there could arise the question of free will. If all *basic concepts that underpin existence* are offshoots of Infinitum Perfectus and pure nothingness, and themselves defined by their exact opposites, along with the fact that everything within existence reacts and is defined by its surroundings – does this then leave room for randomness to occur within existence? Free will of course depends upon the idea of randomness to be an actuality, rather than merely a perception.

Randomness would most accurately be described as something that is absolutely unpredictable. If every existing entity's reactions and what they are specifically reacting to can all be predicted, then this would suggest that every individual entity is predisposed to reacting in a certain way, rather than using actual free will. This does not mean that something is unpredictable if no one on Earth could predict a certain occurrence. The idea of randomness we are looking at is an occurrence that could not be predicted under any circumstance by any form of intelligence.

Predictability

To investigate the concept of randomness we will use examples that are familiar to us, such as rolling a pair of dice or plucking a numbered ball from a lottery barrel. Although it is fairly improbable that any human could accurately predict (as opposed to making a lucky guess) the number drawn from a lottery barrel, or the outcome of a dice roll, those outcomes could be predicted.

When rolling a pair of dice, the outcome could in fact be predicted if someone had the appropriate information, such as: position of dice when thrown, the force used to throw the dice, the height from the ground the dice is thrown, the texture of the surface the dice is thrown upon, the size and texture of the dice, the effects that gravity will have on the dice and several other factors. This isn't limited to something as simple as rolling a pair of dice. No matter how complex a process, the outcome can be theoretically predicted.

Even pulling a numbered ball from a lottery barrel could be predicted if someone had enough information, such as: the number and size of the balls in the barrel, the order in which the balls were put into the barrel, the speed and number of rotations of the barrel, the individual or mechanism that plucks the ball from the barrel and most likely many other factors. Although the information needed to predict a dice roll or a lottery outcome could be beyond any human at present, it does not change the fact that they could be predicted. What must be remembered is that a human's ability to predict a certain outcome, which is not likely in regards to the previous examples mentioned, does not determine that outcome's ability to be theoretically predicted.

Someone may suggest that certain actions or behaviors must be considered random. Such examples could include an individual's decision to scratch their nose, or the apparently random choice one makes in guessing a number on a roulette wheel. The point at which someone scratches their nose, although unlikely to be predicted by any human, could still in theory be predicted if an individual had enough relevant information. Such information would take into consideration the physical and mental tolerance of the individual, along with the severity of the irritation that caused the individual's nose to become itchy. The physical tolerance level would take into account the amount of irritation felt by the individual. The mental tolerance level would then take into account how much pain or irritation that individual can withstand before taking physical action. The force and speed the individual would use to scratch their nose could also be predicted by taking into account the above factors, along with the individual's personality and immediate circumstances. This is relatively similar to predicting the outcome of a dice roll.

The apparently random choice of picking a number, let's say a number between 1 and 100, may appear to be quite a different situation. Some may say that this could only ever be a random choice. Although perhaps a little more complex than the predictability of when and how someone decides to scratch themselves, picking a number between 1 and 100 follows the same basic principles. Many factors would contribute to why an individual would consciously or subconsciously pick a certain number. Certain numbers may have known personal or cultural significances, but quite often the reasoning would be more complex. There would be the mixing of personally significant numbers with numbers that were most recently on the individual's mind for various reasons, in order to generate what would appear to be a random number. Of course the number could come solely from the last number the individual had encountered, or merely a personally significant number. This, however, could feel like a conscious rather than a supposedly random choice.

Further factors would also need to be known in order to accurately predict the number between 1 and 100 an individual would choose, such as: the individual's personal experience, cultural background, their current thoughts and feelings, their thinking process, their immediate situation, and most likely a host of other influences. All of these factors would be difficult for the individual to be consciously aware of, let alone another individual, nevertheless it would still be possible to predict for an entity with intelligence far above our own. So although an individual's choice of picking a number between 1 and 100 would appear random to us, it is in fact not random at all. We often see the idea of randomness, but this is again due to our own limitations.

The idea that everything is theoretically predictable not only raises doubts over free will, but also the idea of the multiverse, which is another concept that often features in discussions of existence. The reason why predictability affects the idea of the multiverse will soon be explained, but we will first address its consequences on free will.

The Question of Free Will

As previously mentioned for true free will to exist it would mean that individual ideas and actions were not predetermined responses by internal predispositions to external stimuli. Individuals need the ability to have alternative responses to the exact same external influences if free will were to be an actuality.

At first many will say that although individuals may be emotionally predisposed to acting in certain ways in certain situations, an individual's intelligence and reason can overcome such predispositions. The thing that everyone needs to remember is that every part of any individual has evolved through a specific set of circumstances in the form of an infinite number of external influences and interactions. For a human these parts would include their physical form, emotions, and their intellect to name but three. All these attributes have and can only have been formed by an infinite number of external influences and interactions. As these influences are derived from predictable concepts, the influences themselves must also act in a patterned and predictable way. Nothing, whether it is someone's emotions, their intellect or any other attribute, can literally form or change randomly. Therefore if someone consciously ignored their emotional impulses and instead acted with intellectual 'reason', this would still be a predictable reaction. In other words, as both intelligence (reason) and emotions are formed in completely predictable, nonrandom ways, then these attributes themselves will be just as predictable.

Even if all actions and reactions can be currently predicted, was there ever the possibility that randomness played a part in existence? One could possibly surmise that at least the very first action in existence was in some way random. This then got existence started off, leading to the predictability of future actions and reactions. If not already obvious, there is a reason why this cannot be the case.

On close examination we can see that there are not in fact actions and reactions; there are only a continual and infinite series of reactions. As there was no first cause or literal beginning to all existence then there could never be a first action. From any existing individual's point of view there could only have been an infinite series of (predictable) reactions based upon fundamental concepts/laws that have always existed. There will also be an infinite series of (predictable) reactions that will occur in the future based upon these same fundamental concepts. As previously stated these concepts are objective truths which cannot be changed.

True free will should be thought of as an action rather than a reaction, as free will requires a random occurrence that goes beyond the infinite series of reactions that occur throughout all existence. As an act of true free will has to come about beyond the infinite series of predictable reactions, this would effectively create something entirely new, randomly out of nothing, which is of course impossible. Even a seemingly unimportant decision about whether someone wanted fettuccine for dinner rather than spaghetti comes about via a series of predictable reactions. This applies to simple human behavior, such as an individual scratching their nose or whether or not someone consciously or unconsciously acts 'morally' or not. This is true for absolutely all entities, whether they are far less or far more evolved than us.

Although free will cannot literally exist, no individual entity will experience the sensation of not having free will. Even if an individual can theoretically understand that free will does not literally exist, the important thing is that all individuals will subjectively feel that free will does exist.

The Multiverse

Obviously if randomness could not occur due to the way the *basic concepts that underpin existence* work, then the idea of the multi-verse would be moot, unless all these universes existed parallel to us in the exact same way. For any theoretical parallel universe or dimension to be different to our own, something random would need to occur to begin the process of making such a dimension different to our own.

From the *basic concepts that underpin existence* to the actuality of our known physical universe and beyond, a step-by-step endless stream of predictable reactions have and will occur. Each concept has a predictable pattern that leads to further and more specific concepts, which is an idea that will be discussed a little more in the last chapter. The actuality of existence also follows a similar pattern, as it is literally formed by these very same concepts. As there is nothing that can lead to a completely unpredictable, random concept to exist, nor anything in the actuality of existence to create a truly random element or occurrence, then any theoretical parallel dimension could only be the exact same as ours.

Rather than thinking that other dimensions consist of humans that are slightly different to us due to some random occurrence, other dimensions should be thought of in a hierarchal fashion.

The reason why another dimension is beyond our capacity to see or consciously interact with is that it is a 'realm' consisting of entities that are either far more or far less evolved than us. There is, however, no literal 'realm' that is hidden from our view by a mystical veil, which we could actually visit if only we could discover its location. Rather these entities' lack of evolution or superior evolution puts them beyond our limited perceptions, so therefore in a sense they could be thought of as occupying the same 'space' as us.

As existence is infinite there will always be, no matter how advanced an individual, other entities that are far inferior and far superior to such an extent that their existence will be beyond comprehension. Therefore rather than the idea of a multiverse, where each universe must exist in exactly the same fashion to our own, we should think in terms of dimensions that are hierarchal on the evolutionary ladder.

The Mystery of Time

What is Time?

There is an idea in science, which has also taken hold in much of Western popular culture, that time is the 4th dimension and that there is in existence a time line that can be theoretically traversed. Time could be seen like a tunnel that could potentially be (time) travelled up and down throughout the 'history of time'. The question that needs to be asked is what exactly is time, or more appropriately the appearance of time? For us humans in our everyday lives we usually judge time by our clocks, in relation to the movement of the Earth around the Sun. Therefore time appears to pass by at the same rate while we're on Earth no matter what we do. There is of course the expression 'time flies when you're having fun', which suggests the appearance of time can alter subjectively.

The important thing to realize when an individual is interpreting the rate in which time appears to travel is that they are in fact experiencing an array of internal reactions. Rather than time moving at different speeds for different people, one individual is consciously experiencing more internal reactions than another individual. The more one is aware of their own internal reactions, or experiences, the slower 'time' will appear.

The expression 'time flies when you're having fun' is really in reference to someone experiencing their internal reactions differently than someone having a bad time. An individual having a bad time is more likely to focus on their pain and misery, as such experiences are difficult not to notice. On the other hand someone experiencing a good time, especially if they are in a heightened state of ecstasy, will be less focused on their purely physical existence, with all its aches and pains. As individuals learn from difficult experiences it is only logical that they should be more consciously aware of their internal reactions during such experiences.

Although 'time' is often labeled as an illusion for those that already disbelieve in the idea of time, it is perhaps not exactly an illusion, but rather a misconception. It is not a complete illusion as the appearance of time is being expressed by something real: an endless sea of reactions, witnessed and experienced by all individual entities. Therefore time should be thought of as a simple misconception.

The Beginning of 'Time'

As you may have already surmised there cannot be a true 'beginning of time'. This is not only because there is no actual time; there is of course no literal beginning to anything, in so much as something appears randomly into existence from nothing. Therefore there cannot even be a beginning of the 'appearance of time'. There is only the appearance of beginnings in specific contexts, such as the subjective beginning of our known physical universe. This of course means that if it were possible to look back into the past, there would be literally no end to how far back you could look. As previously discussed the idea of continued existence does not allow for an absolute beginning, only the idea of subjective beginnings.

Chapter 5

Tiers and Endless Knowledge

Tiers

The concepts that allow for all existence can be grouped into tiers, as seen in the table below. Only the first three tiers are shown as we are only displaying some of the main concepts discussed in this book. These are in fact some of the most important *basic concepts that underpin existence,* which can help generate a pattern to establish lower (more specific) tiers and further concepts that underpin existence.

Infinitum Perfectus			Tier 1
Absolute Good / Perfection (Best)	Evolution (Growth)	Infinity (∞)	Tier 2
Fastest (Faster)	Biggest (Bigger)	White (light and color)	Tier 3

Pure Nothingness			Tier 1
Absolute Evil / Imperfection (Worst)	De-Evolution (Regression)	Absolute Zero (0)	Tier 2
Slowest (Slower)	Smallest (Smaller)	Black (light and color)	Tier 3

Pure nothingness and Infinitum Perfectus are of course in tier 1 as their duality is the prime cause of all existence. One is basically complete nonexistence, while the other allows for the existence of everything possible. For Infinitum Perfectus to occur it needs several basic concepts underneath it to make it a theoretical actuality.

Concepts of the absolute good (perfection) along with the concepts of evolution and infinity are directly tied to Infinitum Perfectus, as Infinitum Perfectus could never be without those three basic concepts. Infinitum Perfectus must be equal to infinity to be the exact opposite of pure nothingness, which is a complete absence of anything. It requires the concept of the absolute good (perfection) otherwise it would not be perfect. It also needs the concept of evolution (growth) in order for its infinite journey to perfection to take place. These are the first and logical requirements for Infinitum Perfectus to juxtapose itself against pure nothingness. Additionally concepts such as de-evolution or regression, and absolute evil (imperfection) can be seen as the journey to pure nothingness. The concept of absolute zero (0) is effectively akin to pure nothingness as it also represents a complete absence, much like the concept of black, which is an absence of light.

Concepts such as the smallest and the biggest, along with the fastest and the slowest, make up the details of evolution so to speak. The concept of light is really a physical representation of the level of perfection reached by an individual. Although some may argue that light should fall under tier 2, as it deals with absence and perfection, we feel that it is a byproduct of the concept of perfection, rather than its equal. All of these tier 3 concepts incorporate infinity, as do all forms of absolute dualities, for there are an infinite amount of variations between two such absolutes, whether it's: shades of light (color), numerals, physical size, speed, sound frequency (vibration), and so on.

The concepts of masculinity and femininity are more likely to fall under tier 4 or lower. Although the principles of masculinity and femininity are considered opposites, they are not extreme opposites in a way that one is considered positive while the other is considered negative. Both concepts would be considered to be a mix of both positive and negative elements. This is unlike the higher tiers that incorporate extreme absolutes, such as absolute zero (0) and infinity (∞), which deal with ideas of absence and perfection. Of course not all absolutes deal with absence and perfection. Infinite speed and absolute stillness do; however, concepts of the fastest and the slowest, along with the biggest and the smallest do not, and yet they are still considered complete absolutes. They, much like the highest and the lowest sound (vibration) frequencies, are still extreme opposites. This is because, in evolutionary terms, the most negative aspect is at one end of the spectrum and the most positive at the other, with an infinite number of variations in between. Therefore masculinity and femininity cannot be considered extreme absolutes, repre-sented by the first 3 tiers.

As you could probably surmise, the lower the tier the more specific the concepts become; while the higher, with Infinitum Perfectus and pure nothingness the highest tier, the broader the concepts are. The more knowledge an individual acquires the more detail one will have of concepts that underpin the whole of existence, subsequently allowing for even further tiers to be revealed.

Obviously the fundamental reason for existence, the concepts of pure nothingness and Infinitum Perfectus defining one another, would be considered the most important parts of existence. Despite this the other basic concepts should be considered just as important. They in effect give the concept of Infinitum Perfectus more depth and detail, albeit in a basic fashion. Such depth is not only important to better understand how existence on the whole works, but also in helping to better understand our immediate Earthly existence.

Future Knowledge

With any new topic of learning it is important to learn the basics, as they underpin everything else. Without explaining how the basics of mathematics work, someone may struggle to utilize mathematics if they had only a brief description of what mathematics was. The same can be said about existence, and specifically Infinitum Perfectus. To merely describe it as 'infinite perfection' would not be useful to many individuals. Once an individual grasps the basics of mathematics they can then see patterns and increase their knowledge of mathematics from there. Knowledge about existence works in the same way. Once the pattern of existence is observed and understood, through the basic explanation of how existence, and specifically Infinitum Perfectus works, then an individual can increase their knowledge of existence by following the established pattern.

Although the *basic concepts that underpin existence* are necessary in explaining how all of existence works, the actuality is that every (nonhuman made) concept is needed for a complete and accurate understanding of all existence. Knowledge of existence can never actually be perfect or complete, but thanks to the law of infinity it can always improve. Therefore there could be an endless stream of literature and ideas discussing existence, becoming more and more specific and detailed. This not only pertains to our current state of existence, but those states of existence which we have already passed through and those that are yet to be discovered.

BOOKS

O is a symbol of the world, of oneness and unity. In different cultures it also means the "eye," symbolizing knowledge and insight. We aim to publish books that are accessible, constructive and that challenge accepted opinion, both that of academia and the "moral majority."

Our books are available in all good English language bookstores worldwide. If you don't see the book on the shelves ask the bookstore to order it for you, quoting the ISBN number and title. Alternatively you can order online (all major online retail sites carry our titles) or contact the distributor in the relevant country, listed on the copyright page.

See our website www.o-books.com for a full list of over 500 titles, growing by 100 a year.

And tune in to myspiritradio.com for our book review radio show, hosted by June-Elleni Laine, where you can listen to the authors discussing their books.

MySpiritRadio